Fodor's

25 Best

BRUSSELS & BRUGES

How to Use This Book

KEY TO SYMBOLS	
✚ Map reference to the accompanying fold-out map	🛳 Nearest riverboat or ferry stop
✉ Address	♿ Facilities for visitors with disabilities
☎ Telephone number	❓ Other practical information
🕐 Opening/closing times	▷ Further information
🍴 Restaurant or café	ℹ Tourist information
🚆 Nearest rail station	✋ Admission charges:
Ⓜ Nearest subway (Metro) station	Expensive (more than €10) Moderate (€6–€9)
🚌 Nearest bus route	Inexpensive (€5 or less)

This guide is divided into four sections

● Essential Brussels and Bruges: An introduction to the cities and tips on making the most of your stay.
● Brussels and Bruges by Area: We've recommended the best sights, shops, entertainment venues, nightlife and restaurants in each city. Suggested walks help you to explore on foot.
● Where to Stay: The best hotels, whether you're looking for luxury, budget or something in between.
● Need to Know: The info you need to make your trip run smoothly, including getting about by public transport, weather tips, emergency phone numbers and useful websites.

Navigation In the Brussels and Bruges by Area chapter, we've given each area its own color, which is also used on the locator maps throughout the book and the map on the inside front cover.

Maps The fold-out map with this book has comprehensive street plans of Brussels and Bruges. The grid on this fold-out map is the same as the grid on the locator maps within the book. We've given grid references within the book for each sight and listing.

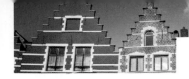

Contents

CONTENTS

Introducing Brussels and Bruges

Brussels and Bruges represent the twin identities of contemporary Belgium. Brussels is the larger, busier city—and Europe's political capital. Bruges, in Flanders, is one of Europe's best-preserved medieval cities and Belgium's tourist capital.

Brussels is a cosmopolitan city; the population was already divided into Flemish and French speakers, but to these are now added the babel of European languages, with English as a common denominator. Speak to anyone who has lived here for a while and they will tell you that it is a very pleasant city to be in, with its wonderful museums, splendid architecture, delightful green spaces, excellent, reasonably priced restaurants and a lively nightlife.

The heart of the city has been restored and revitalized. The district around rue Dansaert, close to the Grand Place, has become a fashionable spot to live or hang out in and nearby streets, such as rue des Chartreux and chaussée de Flandres, regularly see the opening of another hip boutique or restaurant. Other areas are also undergoing a revival, as young European professionals choose to live in the gorgeous art nouveau districts of Ixelles and St.-Gilles, rather than in the suburbs.

Bruges attracts nearly 8 million visitors each year. Flemish is the local language, although most people also know enough English to communicate with visitors. The heart of the city is small and most sights are within walking distance. If you don't want to walk, do as the locals do and go by bicycle.

Unlike Brussels, Bruges spent the last decades trying to keep its look medieval. The Concertgebouw, which opened in 2002, was the first statement that contemporary architecture could have a place here. Now there is a desire to create a broader environment where today's artists can be inspired by the city's rich past.

FACTS AND FIGURES

● There are a staggering 138 restaurants for every square mile (2.6sq km) in Brussels.
● Brussel's Grand Palace is one of several UNESCO World Heritage Sites in the city and Bruges is a UNESCO World Heritage City.
● More than 150 monuments in Bruges have been protected.

BRUSSELS DISTRICTS

The heart of Brussels is enclosed by the "Petit Ring," which more-or-less follows the 14th-century city walls. The Lower Town, near the Grand Place, is where the working classes lived. Now fashionable, it has great restaurants and bars. The French-speaking upper classes lived, and many still do, on the hill, the Upper Town. This area has a lot of grand buildings.

CITY OF BRIDGES

No name is more appropriate than *Brugge*, the Flemish word for bridges. The city had its origins by a bridge over the canal *(reie)*, most probably the Blinde Ezelbrug (Blind Donkey Bridge). To protect the crossing, a borough was built around the bridge and the city grew around it. Bruges still counts many canals and about 50 bridges which help create the city's sense of romance.

CITY OF BUREAUCRATS

Brussels is home not only to the national government of Belgium, but also to the parliaments of two of the country's three regions: Flanders and the Brussels-Capital Region (the third parliament for the region of Wallonia sits in the city of Namur). It also houses the headquarters of NATO and is the official seat of the European Parliament.

A Short Stay in Brussels and Bruges

DAY 1 BRUSSELS

Morning Start the day early at the **Grand Place** (▷ 26), admiring all the superb Gothic facades as well as the tower of the **Hôtel de Ville** (▷ 28). Rub the bronze plaque of Charles Buls, just off the square, for good luck and continue to **Manneken-Pis** (▷ 29). Stroll along **rue Antoine Dansaert** (St.-Géry and Ste.-Catherine, ▷ 38) to get familiar with Belgian fashion and stop for some oysters and a glass of white wine on **place Ste.-Catherine** (▷ 38). Check out avant-garde contemporary art at **CENTRALE** (▷ 36).

Lunch Have a *Bruxellois* lunch at one of the many restaurants on the Chaussée de Flandres, particularly **Viva M'Boma** (▷ 46) or at **Vismet** (▷ 46) for the freshest fish and seafood.

Afternoon Head for the **Sablon** (▷ 35) and enjoy a coffee on a heated terrace, before a serious dip into both old and modern art at the **Musées Fin-de-Siecle and Old Masters** (▷ 30, 32), founded by Napoleon in 1801. Browse in the antiques shops or take in another museum if you can. The wonderful **Musée des Instruments de Musique** (▷ 31) is a good choice—the collection of musical instruments here is one of the most important of its kind in the world and it has great views from its roof terrace. End the afternoon with a stroll through the **Parc de Bruxelles** (▷ 34), once the hunting ground of Belgian kings and now a haven for *Bruxellois* and visitors alike, with its tree-lined avenues and fountain.

Dinner See the Grand Place (▷ 26) by night, take a walk through the **Galeries Royales St.-Hubert** (▷ 40) and eat in a typical Brussels brasserie: the **Taverne du Passage, Vincent** or the grander **Belga Queen** (▷ all 44–46). After dinner have a nightcap at one of the bars on **place St.-Géry** (▷ 38) or at **l'Archiduc** (▷ 42).

DAY 2 BRUGES

Morning Start the day with a delicious breakfast at one of Bruges' many patisseries as you make your way to the Markt (▷ 76). Here take in the impressive Belfry, rising 83m (272ft) above the town. If it is a clear day, climb up for sweeping views over the city and surrounding countryside. Back down again, a narrow street leads to the even more perfect square of **Burg** (▷ 68), with the fine Gothic facade of the **Town Hall** and the **Basiliek Van Het Heilig-Bloed** (▷ 83), where a service for the Adoration of the Holy Blood still takes place every Friday morning. Pass the **Vismarkt** (▷ 86) and walk along de Dijver to the **Groeninge Museum** (▷ 72), with its superb collection of Flemish Primitives.

Lunch Have a typical Belgian lunch at **Den Dyver** (▷ 91), which serves traditional dishes cooked with beer.

Afternoon Continue to the **Begijnhof** (▷ 66) and enjoy the tranquility of the nearby Minnewater (Lovers' Lake). Walk through the small alleys to the old **St.-Janshospitaal** (▷ 80), an interesting building in itself, which houses a fine collection of Hans Memling's paintings. Opposite the medieval hospice rises the large brick tower of the **Onze-Lieve-Vrouwekerk** (▷ 78), with Michelangelo's statue of *Madonna and Child* and other treasures. Stroll through the garden to the **Gruuthuse Museum** (▷ 74) next door. If you have any time left, take a **canal cruise** (▷ 70), starting from just opposite the museum, or ride a *koets* (horse-drawn carriage) through town from the Burg.

Dinner In the evening linger over dinner. Famed for its mussels and lobster dishes, **Breydel De Coninc** (▷ 91) is a favorite with locals. Or try the popular Belgian bistro, **Christophe** (▷ 91). If you fancy a nightcap, head to neighboring bar to sample numerous Belgian beers.

► ► ► BRUSSELS

Centre Belge de la Bande Dessinée ▷ **24–25** A must-see for comic strip *aficionados*.

Grand Place ▷ **26–27** Admire the imposing mix of architectural brilliance in Brussels' famous square.

Heysel ▷ **98–99** Home of the 1958 World Exhibition, with its landmark Atomium.

De Vesten en Poorten ▷ **82** These city fortifications have protected Bruges for more than 600 years.

St.-Janshospitaal en Memling Museum ▷ **80–81** Hans Memling's artworks, housed in an ancient hospice.

Onze-Lieve-Vrouwekerk ▷ **78–79** Magnificent 13th-century church with important medieval art.

Markt ▷ **76–77** Since the 13th century, this market square has been central to Bruges' activities.

Kathedraal St.-Salvator ▷ **75** A 13th-century place of worship containing sculptures and art.

Gruuthuse Museum ▷ **74** A glorious medieval palace with an interesting museum.

Groeninge Museum ▷ **72–73** Flemish art from the 15th century to today.

Damme ▷ **96–97** Just 6.5km (4 miles) outside Bruges, this lovely little town is worth a visit.

Choco-Story ▷ **71** Learn all there is to know about chocolate, and then taste the product.

These pages are a quick guide to the Top 25 sights, described in more detail later. Here they are listed alphabetically, starting with the sights in Brussels and followed by those in Bruges. The tinted background shows which area each sight is in.

Hôtel de Ville ▷ 28
Brussels has the most elegant of all Belgium's Gothic town halls.

Jardin Botanique Meise ▷ 100–101 One of the largest botanical gardens in the world.

Manneken-Pis ▷ 29
Brussels' diminutive bronze statue of a small boy continues to draw crowds.

Musée Fin-de-Siecle ▷ 30 Home to modern Belgian art.

Musée Horta ▷ 52–53
Art nouveau at its absolute best is on show at Victor Horta's former home.

Musée des Instruments de Musique ▷ 31 See musical instruments from across the globe.

Musée Old Masters ▷ 32–33 Don't miss the classical art housed here.

Parc du Cinquantenaire ▷ 50–51 Museums, auto exhibitions and monuments are all here, in one place.

Place Royale ▷ 34 An elegant neoclassical square overlooked by imposing palaces and monuments.

Le Sablon ▷ 35 Sit and people-watch on the terraces of the Place du Grand Sablon.

Map labels:
Heysel (Heizel), Jardin Botanique Meise
Bassin Vergote Vergotedok
Parc Albert I-park
KELBERG
Parc Maximilien-park
ENBEEK
Parc Josaphat-park
CENTRAL BRUSSELS 20–46
JEAN
Jardin Botanique Kruidtuin Gesù
ST JOSSE
ST JOOST
TEN NODE
SCHAERBEEK
Centre Belge de la Bande Dessinée
Grand Place (Grote Markt)
Hôtel de Ville
Parc de Bruxelles Park van Brussel
Manneken-Pis
Musée des Instruments de Musique
Musée Fin-de-Siecle
Place Royale
Parc du Cinquantenaire Jubelpark
OUTH RUSSELS 7-62
BRUSSEL
LE SABLON
Musée Old Masters
Parc d'Egmont Egmontpark
Parc Léopold Leopoldspark
LES MAROLLES
ELSENE
ETTERBEEK
ST-GILLIS
St Jacques
ST GILLS
Musée Horta (Hortamuseum)
IXELLES
Parc de Forêt Park van Vorst
ELSENE
REST VORST
BRUSSEL
Cimetière d'Ixelles Begraafplaats van Elsene
Oudenenpark
Bois de la Cambre
Parc Brugmann-park
Parc Montjoie park
UKKEL

Canal Cruise ▷ 70 A wonderful way to explore the city known as the "Venice of the North."

Burg ▷ 68–69 A Medieval square bounded on all sides by impressive buildings of historical note.

Begijnhof ▷ 66–67 This pretty square of houses was home to an all-female pious community.

BRUGES ◄ ◄ ◄

9

Shopping

An obvious souvenir from Belgium, if not a lasting one, is food. Belgium is known for its plain chocolate, which contains only the best cocoa and a very high proportion of it.

A Chocoholic's Dream Destination

Belgians are serious about their chocolate, as is obvious from the number of shops devoted to chocolate in its many shapes, shades and tastes. You can buy good chocolate bars, such as Côte d'Or, in supermarkets, but it's the hand-made chocolates and pralines that stand out. Prices are generally reasonable, but as you might expect, they rise considerably at the high priest of chocolate, Pierre Marcolini (▷ 41). Do as the Belgians do and look for smaller patisseries that make their own, including Spegelaere (▷ 89) and Depla Pol (▷ 88) in Bruges and Mary's (▷ 41) in Brussels.

The Way the Cookie Crumbles

Equally delicious are Belgian cookies such as *speculoos* (slightly spicy biscuits), *pain à la Grècque* (a light biscuit with sugar), *pain d'amandes* (butter biscuit with shaved almonds) and *pain d'épices* (a cake with cinnamon and candied fruits). Destrooper is a good brand and is stocked in supermarkets.

DESIGNER SHOPPING

Brussels is slowly taking over from Antwerp as Belgium's fashion capital. The Brussels tourist office, on Grand Place, has useful information on established and upcoming fashion districts. On Fridays and Saturdays, free shopping buses shuttle between seven city center neighborhoods. In the old St.-Boniface quarter you'll find new designers and stores as well as popular bars and restaurants. Most Belgian designers, including Walter Van Beirendonck, Ann Demeulemeester, Dries Van Noten, Dirk Bikkembergs, Veronique Branquinho and Chris Mestdagh, are available at the Stijl (▷ 41), the store that is the grand temple of Belgian fashion. These designers produce accessible avant-garde fashion, while designers such as Olivier Strelli produce more commercial clothes.

Clockwise from top: A chocolate sculpture by Pierre Marcolini; a shop in the Galeries St. Hubert; Comics

Liquid Refreshment

Beer is another good buy with over 800 labels to choose from. Every bar has a beer menu, so you might want to try a few varieties before deciding which to stock up on. Larger super-markets have a good selection of beers, and beer shops can be found in tourist areas in both cities.

Lace, Tapestry and Fashion

Belgium was famous in the Middle Ages for its tapestry and exquisite lace, and there is still plenty of it for sale, although very little is now handmade in Belgium and what you can find is usually very pricey. Belgian fashion designers enjoy worldwide success, so take a closer look at their work in Brussels, particularly in and around rue Antoine Dansaert. Local designers such as Dries Van Noten, Martin Margiela and Veronique Branquinho create innovative designs based on Belgian traditions.

Art and Comics

Art galleries are all over Brussels—for details obtain a copy of the brochure *Art Brussels* from the tourist office. Many shops specialize in comic books, but none so much as the Tintin shop (▷ 40). Here you can choose from a selection of Tintin books, collectibles, clothes, towels and even wallpaper.

SHOPPING DISTRICTS

The main shopping streets in Bruges are Geldmuntstraat-Noordzandstraat and Steenstraat-Zuidzandstraat. In Brussels, the main shopping street, rue Neuve, has all the international high-street brands and the large shopping mall City 2. The Galeries Royales St.-Hubert (▷ 40) has good traditional shops focusing on design, books, fashion and chocolates. Avenue Louise is Brussels' upscale shop-ping area, with everything from Chanel to the Belgian designer Olivier Strelli. The most popular place to shop, for fashion, is the area around rue Antoine Dansaert (▷ 38, St.-Géry), which has the best shoe shops in Brussels and shops of new designers.

Art Museum interior; Galeries Avenue Louise's; delicastes-sen Diksmuides Boterhuis; Patisserie Mairy

Shopping by Theme

Whether you're looking for a department store, a quirky boutique, or something in between, you'll find it all in Brussels and Bruges. On this page shops are listed by theme. For a more detailed write-up, see the individual listings in Brussels and Bruges by Area.

Brussels and Bruges by Night

The Belgian joke that there's a bar on every corner can't be far from the truth. What's more, licensing laws permit them to stay open as long as they like—often until dawn.

Enjoying a Drink
The bar scene is lively in both cities, as this is what locals do when they go out at night. Even if they go out for dinner or to a show, they still end up having a beer in a bar. The pace of drinking is usually slow but steady, making it easier to keep going all night. In Brussels you can start on the Grand Place, where the view comes at a price. Nearby there are trendy bars around place St.-Géry and rue du Marché au Charbon, as well as pricier establishments around Le Sablon. Look in Les Marolles or St.-Gilles for traditional *Bruxellois* cafés. For jazz clubs and wine bars, try Ixelles.

An Evening Stroll
In Brussels, head for the Grand Place, beautifully floodlit at night. In Bruges, the liveliest areas are the Eiermarkt and 't Zand and the canals are well lit.

Outdoor Living
In summer, Belgians spend long evenings sitting on café terraces chatting. The best in Brussels include Le Roy d'Espagne, La Lunette, Le Falstaff (▷ 45) and the café terraces on the place du Grand Sablon. In Bruges, most people head for cafés on Eiermarkt and 't Zand.

From top: Relaxing in Bruges; enjoy live music on your trip; the Markt at night in Bruges; Arc de Triomphe in Brussels

---

WHAT'S ON

The English-language weekly *The Bulletin* (thebulletin.be) has a "What's On" supplement, or pick up one of the free city guides, like *Agenda* (agenda.brussels.be) in Brussels, or *Exit* in Bruges which has entertainment listings in French or Flemish. In Brussels, tickets to events can be bought from FNAC (in City 2, rue Neuve ☎ 02 275 1111), the tourist office on the Grand Place or the venue; in Bruges, from the tourist office in Concertgebouw, on 't Zand (☎ 050 444 646).

Where to Eat

Belgians love to eat and they do it well. Brussels and Bruges have no shortage of excellent restaurants offering Belgian and international fare, prepared with fresh ingredients and served in simple but convivial surroundings. This is true for most eateries, from the simple bistro to the ultimate palace of haute cuisine.

Belgian Dishes

Contrary to popular belief, there is more to Belgian food than *moules frites*. *Waterzooi* is a little-known national dish, a delicate green stew of fish or chicken with leeks, parsley and cream. Plain but delicious, *stoemp* is potatoes mashed with vegetables, often served with sausages. *Carbonnade flamande* is beef braised in beer with carrots and thyme, and *lapin à la gueuze* is rabbit stewed in gueuze beer with prunes. *Anguilles au vert/paling in het groen* (river eels in green sauce) is another popular dish. A real treat are Belgian waffles, eaten with icing sugar, whipped cream or fruit.

Vegetarian Choices

Belgians like their meat, but options are available for vegetarians. For those who eat it, there is always plenty of fish on the menu. Salads are a popular choice for lunch and vegetarians will find plenty of meat-free dishes in ethnic restaurants, as well as in some specifically vegetarian restaurants. For vegetarian restaurant suggestions in Brussels (▷ 62). In Bruges, try De Plaats (▷ 92).

FRITES, FRITES, FRITES

Belgium claims the best fries in the world. The secret of their *frites* is that they are fried twice and thrown into the air to get rid of the extra oil. Every Belgian has a preferred *friture* or *frietkot*, but most agree that Maison Antoine (▷ 62), on Place Jourdain in Brussels, and the Friterie de la Barriere St.-Gilles, at Avenue du Parc in St.-Gilles 3, are the best. In Bruges, have a cone of piping hot *frieten* from the *frietkot* on the Markt.

Belgium is famous for its beer and frites—*both can be enjoyed in bustling bars*

Where to Eat by Cuisine

There are places to eat to suit all tastes and budgets in Brussels and Bruges. On this page they are listed by cuisine. For a more detailed description of each venue, see Brussels and Bruges by Area.

Bars and Cafés
Brussels
Brasserie Verschueren
  (▷ 60)
Café Belga (▷ 60)
Le Cercle des Voyageurs
  (▷ 44)
Daringman (▷ 45)
Le Falstaff (▷ 45)

Bruges
'T Brugs Beertje (▷ 91)
Café Vlissinghe (▷ 91)
L'Estaminet (▷ 91)
De Republiek (▷ 92)

Belgian and Brasseries
Brussels
Au Vieux Bruxelles
  (▷ 60)
Belga Queen (▷ 44)
Le Clan des Belges
  (▷ 60)
Le Framboisier Doré
  (sorbets; ▷ 62)
Maison Antoine (▷ 62)
La Mer du Nord (▷ 45)
Le Pain Quotidien
  (▷ 46)
Taverne du Passage
  (▷ 46)
L'Ultime Atome (▷ 62)
Vincent (▷ 46)

Bruges
Breydel de Coninc
  (▷ 91)
Cafedraal (▷ 91)
Christophe (▷ 91)
Den Dyver (▷ 91)
Jan van Eyck (▷ 92)
De Plaats (▷ 92)
De Stove (▷ 92)

Best Dining
Brussels
La Belle Maraîchère
  (▷ 44)
Comme Chez Soi
  (▷ 44)
La Manufacture
  (▷ 45)
La Quincaillerie (▷ 62)
Rouge Tomate (▷ 62)
Vismet (▷ 46)
Viva M'Boma (▷ 46)

Bruges
Bistro Bruut (▷ 91)
Den Gouden Harynck
  (▷ 92)

International
Brussels
Aux Mille et Une Nuits
  (*Tunisian;* ▷ 60)
Bocconi (*Italian;* ▷ 44)
Bonsoir Clara
  (*Mediterranean;*
  ▷ 44)
Comocomo (*tapas;*
  ▷ 45)
Divino (*Italian;* ▷ 45)
La Kasbah (*Moroccan;*
  ▷ 45)
Le Fils de Jules
  (*Basque;* ▷ 61)
L'Horloge du Sud
  (*West African;* ▷ 62)
Little Asia (*Vietnamese;*
  ▷ 45)

Bruges
De Florentijnen (*Italian;*
  ▷ 92)
Rock Fort
  (*Mediterranean;*
  ▷ 92)
Tanuki (*Japanese;* ▷ 92)

Top Tips For...

These great suggestions will help you tailor your ideal visit to Brussels and Bruges, no matter how you choose to spend your time. Each sight or listing has a fuller write-up elsewhere in the book.

A LAZY MORNING
Immerse yourself in the flea market at place du Jeu de Balle in the Marolles district of Brussels (▷ 37) on a Sunday morning.
Linger over a coffee and a delicious pastry at Le Pain Quotidien (▷ 46) in Brussels.
Walk through the park that covers the old city walls around Bruges (▷ 82).

ART NOUVEAU ARCHITECTURE
Head for Victor Horta's own house in Brussels, now the splendid Horta Museum (▷ 52–53).
Rent a bicycle and cycle past Brussels' many art nouveau monuments (▷ 56).
Visit a museum: The Musée des Instruments de Musique (▷ 31) or the Centre Belge de la Bande Dessinée (▷ 24) are both superb examples of Brussels' art nouveau architecture.

SHOPPING SPREES
For Belgian fashion head for Stijl (▷ 41) and other stores in Brussels' rue Antoine Dansaert and the surrounding area.
For designer labels Brussels' avenue Louise is your ticket to paradise.
For antiques visit the weekend antiques market on the Sablon (▷ 35).
For the story of chocolate visit The Chocolate Line in Bruges (▷ 88) and indulge.

ROMANTIC EVENING STROLLS
Take in the Grand Place, one of the most beautiful squares in Europe and which is spectacularly lit at night (▷ 26–27).
Walk along the inner canals in the heart of Bruges (▷ 70); they'll lead you away from the shopping streets to peace and quiet.

Clockwise from top: Marolles flea market; boat on Bruges' Groenerei; the flower market on Grand Place; the kitchen

CHOCOLATES

Visit the high temple of chocolate, Pierre Marcolini's grand and stylish shop (▷ 41) on the Place du Grand Sablon in Brussels.

Learn about the history of chocolate and how the Belgian pralines are made at Bruges' Choco-Story (▷ 71).

Taste the best chocolates, handmade in small patisseries such as Spegelaere (▷ 89) in Bruges and Mary's (▷ 41) in Brussels.

CULTURE TRAILS

Admire the Flemish Primitives in all their glory at the Groeninge Museum (▷ 72–73) and Hans Memling Museum (▷ 80–81) in Bruges and in Brussels at the Musée Old Masters (▷ 32–33).

Take time to view the facades of each house on the Grand Place in Brussels (▷ 26–27), where the statues and ornate carvings on the guildhalls tell many a fascinating story.

Explore some of Brussels' historic squares, especially Place Royale (▷ 34) and the Sablon district (▷ 35), enjoying the passing scene from one of the terrace cafés.

Hitch a ride on one of the canal boats in Bruges (▷ 70) to understand why the city is known as "Venice of the North."

Go to church to admire the sculptures and tapestries in the Kathedraal St.-Salvator, a landmark in Bruges (▷ 75), and don't miss the exquisite *Madonna and Child* by Michelangelo amid the great Gothic architecture of Onze-Lieve-Vrouwekerk (▷ 78–79).

BELGIAN CUISINE

Try the surprising offal dishes at one of Brussels' most acclaimed restaurants, Viva M'Boma (▷ 46).

Join the locals at the popular all-Belgian brasserie Belga Queen (▷ 44); in Bruges try all-day dining at Jan van Eyck (▷ 92).

Enjoy the ultimate Belgian culinary delights at the two-Michelin-star Comme Chez Soi (▷ 44), but reserve well in advance.

at Comme Chez Soi; take an evening stroll in Bruges' Markt; facade of the Musée des Instruments de Musique

ESSENTIAL BRUSSELS AND BRUGES TOP TIPS FOR…

STAYING IN LUXURY

Rocco Forte's Amigo Hotel (▷ 112) hits the right spot—a stylish, luxurious hotel with immaculate service, located right next to Brussels' Grand Place.

The Warwick Barsey in Brussels (▷ 112) offers stylish yet homey luxury and is close to the shops.

De Orangerie (▷ 112) is one of Bruges' most romantic hotels, in a 15th-century convent next to one of the city's most beautiful canals.

INTIMATE HOTELS

Hotel Montanus (▷ 111) in Bruges is a charming boutique hotel located in a 17th-century mansion.

Le Dixseptième, in a great location in Brussels (▷ 112), offers charming rooms in a beautifully restored 17th-century building.

OPERA AND DANCE

Witness world-class opera and marvel at the opulent decor at the national opera house of Théâtre Royal de la Monnaie (▷ 38), in Brussels.

Watch and hear local and international dance and music at Bruges' Concertgebouw (▷ 83), the city's 21st-century landmark.

KEEPING THE KIDS HAPPY

Buy fashion by mainly Belgian designers from the kids' store of Stijl (▷ 41) and Kat en Muis, at rue du Vieux Marché aux Grains 35 in Brussels.

Hit the rides at the theme park Walibi (▷ 106).

Watch the dolphins and enjoy the fairground at the Boudewijn Seapark in Bruges (▷ 102).

Come face to face with dinosaurs at the Museum des Sciences Naturelles (▷ 55).

Enter a Smurf house at the Centre Belge de la Bande Dessinée (▷ 24).

Delight in the costumes in the Garderobe Mannekenpis (▷ 29), it's free to under-18s.

Explore the EU in miniature at Bruparck (▷ 102).

From top: Luxury hotels; the Théâtre Royal de la Monnaie; rides at Six Flags; the Museum of Natural Sciences

Brussels and Bruges by Area

Central Brussels

The Lower Town, around the Grand Place, is the historical heart of Brussels. The Upper Town, on a steep hill, is home to royalty, state institutions and art museums.

3

Place et Square Saincteletteplein en square
Place de l'Yser IJzerplein
BOULEVARD BAUDO
BOULEVARD D'ANVE
Yser / IJzer
Rue des Commercants
Quai au Foin
K.V.S Théâtre
Ypres / Ieper
QUAI AU COMMERCE
Quai aux Pierres de Taille
BD DU 9E DE LIGNE
Caserne du Petit Château
Rue du Canal Vaartstraat
Rue du Canal
Petit Château / Klein Kasteeltje
BD DU NIEUPORT
Hospital Pacheco
Rue Locquenghien
Rue du Grand Hospice
Porte de Flandre / Vlaamsepoort
Rue de Flandre
Rue Antoine
QUAI A BARQUES
QUAI A LA CHAUX
Square des Blindes
Place du Béguinage
Saint Jean-Baptiste

4

BD BATHELEMYLAAN
Place du Nouv Marché aux Grains
Sainte-Catherine / Sint-Katelijne
STE-CATHERINE
Place de Brouckère-plein
Place de la Monnaie
Rue de l'Ec
Rue de Flandre
Place Sainte Catherine Tour Noire
De Brouckère La Monnaie
Place de Ninove Ninoofseplein
Rue Notre Dame du Sommeil
Rue de la Braie
Sainte Catherine
CENTRALE
Théâtre Royal de la Monnaie
DANSAERTSTRAAT
Porte de Ninove / Ninoofsepoort
Rue des Fabriques
ST-GÉRY
Bourse Beurs
PACHLAAN
BOULEVARD DE L'ABBATTOIR
Place Jardins aux Fleurs
Bourse (Beurs)
Église St-Nicolas
Galéries Royal St-Hubert

5

Arts et Métiers
Rue T Kintstraat
Place St-Géry
BOULEVARD ANS-
Grand Place (Grote Markt) Maison du Roi
Rue de la Blandine
N D à Riches-Claires
Hôtel de Ville
Rue Van Arreveldestraat
Musée de la Ville de Bruxelles
Rue d'Anderlecht
Bon Secours
Rue du Marché du Lombard
Manneken-Pis
Porte d'Anderlecht / Anderlechtspoort
Rue de Cureghem
Rue d'Anderlecht
Gouvern Prov
Place Saint Jean
Anneessens
Rue du Midi
Place de la Vieille Halle aux Blés

6

Bodeghem / Bodegem
Saint Antoine
BOULEVARD M LEMONNIERLAAN
Acad
Place Rouppe-plein
BRUSSEL
Place de Dinant
BD DE L'EMPER
Palais du Midi
CHAPELLE KAPEL
N D de la Chapelle
Mus Fin-de-Siè
Place d u Grd Sablon
Lemonnier
ZUIDLAAN
BOULEVARD DU MIDI
Weydenstraat
Place de la Chapelle
LE SABLON
M Yourcenar Archiv
Rue du Miroir
Conservatoire de Musique
Minimes

7

RUE
N D Immaculée
BLAESSTRAAT
HAUTE
HOOGSTRAAT
M de Breughel
Place Poelaertplein
RUE DES 4 BR
Place du Jeu de Balle
Vieux Marché
Palais de Justice (Justitiepaleis)
Louise Louiz
LES MAROLLES
Porte de Hal Halleport
Hôpital Universitaire Saint Pierre
Porte de Hal Halleport
C
D BOULEVARD

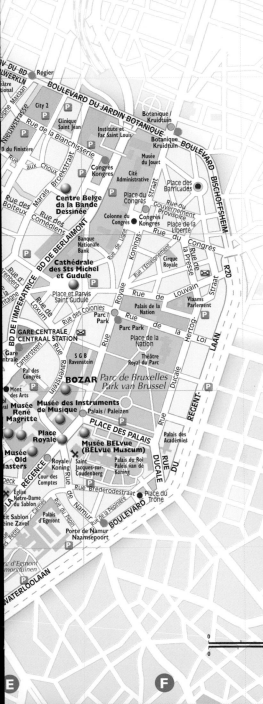

NV DU BD
LWERKIN   Rogier
être
ional

BOULEVARD DU JARDIN BOTANIQUE

City 2

Botanique /
Kruidtuin

Neuwstrasse

Rue de la Blanchisserie

Clinique
Saint Jean

Institute et
Fac Saint Louis

BOULEVARD

BISCHOFFSHEIM

D du Finistère

Rue aux Choux

Rue de
Boteux

Rue des
Comédiens

Marais

Breokstraat

Botanique
Kruidtuin

Musée
du Jouet

Congrès
Kongres

Cité
Administrative

Place des
Barricades

Centre Belge
da la Bande
Dessinée

Colonne du
Congrès

Place du
Congrès

Rue du
Gouvernement
Provisoire

Congrès /
Kongres

Place de la
Liberté

R20

Banque
Nationale
Bank

Rue de Ligne

Konings

Rue de l'Enseignement

Rue

du

Congrès

Rue de
la Presse

BD DE BERLAIMONT

Rue d'
Orenberg

Cathédrale
des Sts Michel
et Gudule

Place et Parvis
Saint Gudule

Royale

Rue

de

Louvain

Cirque
Royale

Hertog

Vlaams
Parlement

straat

BD DE L'IMPERATRICE

Rue de la
Montagne

Rue de
Loxum

Rue des colonies

Parc
Park

Palais de la
Nation

GARE CENTRALE
CENTRAAL STATION

Cantersteen

Ravensteur

Rue

Rue

de

la

Loi

LAAN

Parc Park

Place de la
Nation

Gare
centrale

Pal des
Congrès

S G B
Ravenstein

Théâtre
Royal du Parc

REGENT

Mont
des Arts

BOZAR

Parc de Bruxelles
Park van Brussel

Ducale

al

Musée
René
Magritte

Musée des Instruments
de Musique

Palais / Paleizen

PLACE DES PALAIS

Place
Royale

Musée BELvue
(BELvue Museum)

Palais des
Académies

Rue

Musée
Old
Masters

Royale
Koning

Saint
Jacques-sur-
Coudenberg

Palais du Roi
Palais van de
Koning

DUCALE

RUE

REGENCE

deck

Cour des
Comptes

Rue

de

Namur

Rue de la Pépinière

Place du
Trône

LA

Eglise
Notre-Dame
du Sablon

Rue

du

Pagin

Rue

Camos

Rue Brederodestraat

tit Sablon
eine Zavel

Palais
d'Egmont

BOULEVARD

Porte de Namur
Naamsepoort

d'Egmont
moniuinen

WATERLOOLAAN

0   250 m

0   250 yds

E   F   G

Central Brussels

Centre Belge de la Bande Dessinée

Combining comic strips and the art nouveau architecture for which Brussels is famous, this is one of the city's unusual delights.

Hergé and Tintin The most famous artist and storyteller is Hergé (Georges Remi), with his 1929 creations of Tintin the intrepid reporter and Milou (Snowy) his faithful companion. Hergé was a comic-strip artist long before he invented Tintin and the Hergé Area tells of his work as an illustrator.

Art and invention The collection here includes everything to do with European comics, from the very earliest illustrations to the latest developments in what has become a valued art form in its own right. Permanent exhibitions go back

to the beginning to explore how the comic strip was invented and look at the various forms, genres and styles it takes today.

Meet the Smurfs Behind a gigantic panel of 100 portraits of the Smurfs, the Peyo Exhibition introduces the world of their creator, Pierre Culliford, better known by his pen name, Peyo. While adults enjoy the artwork, children can play in a very realistic Smurf house.

The Magasins Waucquez The collection is housed in the former Waucquez fabric store that opened in 1906 and was designed by Victor Horta. With a sweeping staircase, glass skylights and flower and plant motifs, it is a masterpiece of art nouveau. An exhibition about the building is displayed on the lower floor.

THE BASICS

comicscenter.net

✚ E4

✉ Rue des Sables 20

☎ 02 219 1980

🕐 Daily 10–6

🍴 Restaurant/bar

Ⓖ Gare Centrale/Centraal Station or de Brouckère

🚋 Tram 3, 4, 31, 32, 33

♿ Good

✋ Expensive

Grand Place

HIGHLIGHTS

● Hôtel de Ville (▷ 28)
● La Maison du Roi houses the Museé de la Ville de Bruxelles (▷ 37)
● Elegant dome of Roy d'Espagne
● No. 10 L'Arbre d'Or (Golden Tree) is the Musée des Brasseurs Belges (Belgian Brewer's Museum)
● Daily flower market

In the morning, the sun lights up the gilded Gothic, Renaissance and baroque facades of one of the world's most stunning squares. There is no doubt that this is the heart of Brussels.

Early days By the 11th century, the Grand Place was already humming as a marketplace, and by the 13th century the first three guildhalls had been built here, for the butchers, bakers and clothmakers. The guilds were trade organizations that regulated working conditions and hours, as well as the trade outside the town. As the guilds became increasingly powerful, they even took part in a number of wars, and commanded ever higher membership fees. The guilds' might is never more palpable than when you stand in the Grand Place. Destroyed by a

Clockwise from left: a regal statue crowns the Maison du Roi; horses, flagbearers and pageantry at the vivid Ommegang celebration; a group of life-size Meyboom Puppets pose for a photograph

French bombardment in 1695 (except for the Hôtel de Ville, ▷ 28), the square was entirely rebuilt by the guilds in less than five years.

The guildhalls Each one in the Grand Place is distinguished by statues and ornate carvings. Look for No. 5 La Louve (the She-Wolf), representing the archers' guild; No. 7 Le Renard (Fox), the haberdashers' guild; No. 9 Le Cygne (Swan), the butchers' guild, where Karl Marx and Friedrich Engels wrote *The Communist Manifesto* in 1848; Nos. 24–25 La Chaloupe d'Or (Golden Galleon), the tailors' guild; and Nos. 26–27 Le Pigeon, representing the painters' guild, where novelist Victor Hugo stayed in 1852. Also of interest are Nos. 29–33, the Maison du Roi, called the Broodhuis in Flemish; used by Charles V, which was a bread hall.

Hôtel de Ville

The Gothic frontage (left) of the Hôtel de Ville; a door detail (right)

THE BASICS

✚ E5
✉ Grand Place
☎ 02 513 8940
🕐 Guided tours only, in English; Wed 2pm, Sun 11, 3, 4
🚇 Gare Centrale/Centraal Station or Bourse/Beurs
🚋 Tram 3, 4, 31, 32
♿ Good
✋ Moderate

HIGHLIGHTS

● Grand Staircase
● Bell tower
● Magnificent tapestries

Had architect Jan van Ruysbroeck foreseen how much his elegant bell tower for the Hôtel de Ville would be admired today, perhaps he would not (as legend has it) have thrown himself off it. The Town Hall is a Gothic masterpiece.

A work of art Flanders and Brabant have a wealth of Gothic town halls, but the Brussels Hôtel de Ville is probably the most beautiful of all. It was started in the spring of 1402; the right wing was added in 1444. The octagonal tower, 96m (315ft) high, was added later by architect Jan van Ruysbroeck and bears a gilt statue of the Archangel Michael. The top of the tower, 400 steps up, gives the best views over the Grand Place. Most sculptures adorning the facade of the Town Hall are 19th-century replacements of 14th- and 15th-century originals that are now in the Musée de la Ville de Bruxelles (▷ 37). The courtyard has two 18th-century fountains against the west wall, representing Belgium's most important rivers— the Meuse (to the left) and Scheldt (right).

The Grand Staircase The Grand Staircase carries the busts of all the mayors of Brussels since Belgian independence in 1830. Count Jacques Lalaing painted the murals in 1893.

The Gothic Hall The splendid 16th-century Council Chamber is decorated with lavish 19th-century tapestries depicting the city's main guilds and crafts.

Manneken-Pis

Europe Day celebrations (left); Mannekin uncovered; top photo spot (right)

This statue of a boy may be so small that you might walk straight by him, but he's famous throughout the city.

Cheeky cherub Manneken-Pis is one of Brussels' more amusing symbols. The bronze statuette, less than 2ft (60cm) high, was created by Jerôme Duquesnoy the Elder in 1619. Known then as "Petit Julien," it has since become a legend. One story claims that the Julien on whom the statue was modeled was the son of Duke Gottfried of Lorraine; another alleges that the statue memorializes a boy who urinated on a bomb fuse to save the Town Hall from destruction.

Often vandalized The statue was kidnapped by the English in 1745, as a way of getting at the people of Brussels; two years later the French took him away. In 1817 he was stolen by a French convict and was in pieces when he was recovered. The fragments were used to make the mold for the present statue. Even now he remains a temptation: He has been removed several times by drunk or angry students.

An extravagant wardrobe The French king Louis XV gave him a richly embroidered robe and the cross of Louis XIV as reparation for the bad actions of his soldiers in 1747. Now, Manneken-Pis has some 1,000 costumes and his own museum nearby to house them: Garderobe Mannekenpis, rue du Chêne 19.

THE BASICS

➕ D5

✉ Corner of rue de l'Etuve and rue du Chêne

🚇 Gare Centrale/Centraal Station or Bourse/Beurs

🚌 46, 48, 95; tram 3, 4

🖐 Free

❓ For the dates when Manneken-Pis is dressed up, see the sign at the statue

DID YOU KNOW?

● In 1985, feminists demanded a female version of Manneken-Pis and commissioned Jeanneke-Pis (✉ Impasse de la Fidelité, off rue des Bouchers).
● Every September 13, Manneken-Pis wears the uniform of a sergeant in the Regiment of Welsh Guards to celebrate the liberation of Brussels in 1944.
● The Garderobe Mannekenpis is open Tue–Sun 10–5; free entry 1st Sun of month and to under 18s.

Musée Fin-de-Siècle

TOP 25

Discover modern Belgian art at the Musée Fin-de-Siècle

THE BASICS

fine-arts-museum.be

➕ E6

✉ Rue de la Régence 3

☎ 02 508 3211

🕐 Tue–Fri 10–5, Sat–Sun 11–6

🍽 Cafeteria-restaurant

🚇 Gare Centrale/Centraal Station or Trône/Troon

🚌 27, 38, 60, 71, 95, 96; tram 92, 93

♿ Very good

✋ Expensive (free 1st Wed of month from 1pm)

❓ Regular temporary exhibitions as well as readings and music (see becomeafriend.be)

☎ 02 511 4116)

HIGHLIGHTS

● *Strange Masks*, James Ensor

● *The River Seine at La Grande-Jatte*, Georges Seurat

● *The Nature*, Alphonse Mucha

● *The Bather*, Léon Spillaert

● Gillion Crowet Collection

Exploring the flowering of the arts between the years 1868 and 1914, this involving museum reveals Brussels as Europe's creative crossroads at the turn of the century.

Artistic overview As well as paintings, drawings and sculptures by Belgian and international artists, there are treasures from across the artistic disciplines, from architecture to literature, music to photography, poetry and the decorative arts, all reflecting the great changes that occurred as the centuries turned.

Four inviting floors Housed in the same building as the Musée Old Masters (▷ 32) and Musée Rene Magritte (▷ 38), the Musée Fin-de-Siècle spans four subterranean floors (-5 to -8). The first section is devoted to realism, a style brilliantly reflected in Belgian artist Charles Hermans' *At Dawn* and Louis Artan's forceful seascape *The Wreck*. On the next level down there's a crowd-pleasing collection of paintings by James Ensor and an excellent graphic design section. Symbolism in art and literature follows, with work by Fernand Khnopff.

The decorative arts Featuring an abundance of art nouveau paintings, furniture, ceramics and glass, the fabulous Gillion Crowet Collection on level -8 feels like a museum within a museum. Finally, there's a section devoted to two of Belgium's most-loved artists, Léon Spilliaert and George Minne.

Pianos on display (left); the museum's distinctive art nouveau facade (right)

Musée des Instruments de Musique

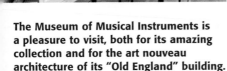

The Museum of Musical Instruments is a pleasure to visit, both for its amazing collection and for the art nouveau architecture of its "Old England" building.

The collection The museum was created in 1877 from two important collections, that of the Belgian musicologist François-Joseph Fétis and the gift to King Leopold II of a large number of Indian musical instruments by Rajah Sourindro Mohun Tagore. Since then the museum has acquired instruments from across the centuries and from all over the world. Today, with more than 7,000 instruments, one quarter of which are on display, it is one of the most important museums of its kind in the world. The bulk of the collection is European, from the Renaissance onward. Every instrument is beautifully displayed, and some are astonishing, like the glass harmonica designed by the American inventor and statesman Benjamin Franklin (1706–90), for which both Beethoven and Mozart wrote music, or the 18th-century *pochettes*, tiny violins that violin teachers could carry in their pockets. As you tour the museum, headsets allow you to listen to each instrument.

Old England Building The Old England Department Store, in which the museum is housed, was designed in 1899 by Paul Saintenoy. Inspired by the British Arts and Crafts movement, he decided upon a grand art nouveau-style building with swirling wrought iron, floral decoration and lots of natural light.

THE BASICS

mim.be

⊞ E6

✉ Rue Montagne de la Cour 2

☎ 02 545 0130

🕐 Tue–Fri 9.30–5, Sat–Sun 10–5

🍴 Bar and restaurant (on top floor, with summer terrace)

🚇 Gare Centrale/Centraal Station or Parc/Park

🚋 Tram 92, 93

♿ Good

💰 Expensive; free 1st Wed of the month after 1pm

❓ Regular lunchtime concerts are held in the 8th-floor Concert Hall; check the MIM website for times and details

DID YOU KNOW?

● Giacomo Puccini died in 1924 in a hospital near the place du Trône, in Brussels.
● Adolphe Sax, the Belgian musician who invented the saxophone in 1846, studied at the Royal Music Conservatoire in Brussels, where Clara Schumann, Hector Berlioz, Niccolò Paganini, Richard Wagner and many others appeared.

Musée Old Masters

HIGHLIGHTS

- *The Fall of the Rebel Angels*, Bruegel the Elder
- *Four Studies of the Head of a Moor* and *The Road to Calvary*, Rubens
- *The King Drinks*, Jacques Jordaens
- *Virgin and Child*, Quentin Metsys
- *The Martyrdom of St Sebastian*, Hans Memling
- *Pietà*, Rogier van der Weyden
- *The Death of Marat*, J-L David

With paintings from the Flemish, Dutch, French and Italian schools, the Old Masters Museum highlights the artistic riches of the 15th to 18th centuries in Europe.

The collection The Musée Old Masters is a treasure house of Flemish art and is one of several museums that collectively form the Musées Royaux de Beaux-Arts de Belgique (Royal Museums of Fine Arts of Belgium), which also includes the Musée Fin-de-Siecle (▷ 30) and the Musée René Magritte (▷ 38).

World famous A tour of the rooms begins with impressive works by the Flemish Primitives Rogier van der Weyden, Hieronymus Bosch, Gerard David, Petrus Christus, Quinten Metsys

From left: Interior of the Musée Old Masters; taking a break while admiring the paintings; the museum's impressive exterior

and particularly Hans Memling. The museum's collection of paintings by the Netherlandish Renaissance artist, Pieter Bruegel the Elder, is internationally renowned.

Rubens and more One large gallery is devoted to Peter-Paul Rubens and displays some powerful portraits and large-scale canvases. En route there you'll find two more famous Flemish Baroque painters, Jacques Jordaens and Antony van Dyck, as well as perhaps the greatest of all Dutch artists, Rembrandt van Rijn.

French Revolution The museum was founded by Napoleon Bonaparte in 1801 and much of the original collection came from forced requisitions during the French Revolution. *The Death of Marat* by Jacques-Louis David, is a highlight.

THE BASICS

fine-arts-museum.be

🚆 E6

✉ Rue de la Régence 3

☎ 02 508 3211

🕐 Tue–Fri 10–5, Sat–Sun 11–6

🍴 Cafeteria-restaurant

🚉 Gare Centrale/Centraal Station or Trône/Troon

🚌 27, 34, 38, 60, 71, 95, 96; tram 92, 93

♿ Good

💵 Expensive (free 1st Wed of month from 1pm)

❓ Regular exhibitions, music and readings (see Friends of the Museum, becomeafriend.be, tel: 02 511 4116)

Place Royale

TOP 25

The Royal Palace's Throne Room (below); statue of Godefroid de Bouillon (right)

THE BASICS

🔁 E6

🚇 Trône/Troon/ Gare Centrale/ Centraal Station

🚊 Tram 92, 94

Église St.-Jacques-sur-Coudenberg

🕐 Tue–Sat 1–5.45, Sun 8.30–5.45

♿ None 💶 Free

Palais Royal

🕐 22 Jul–2 Sep, Tue–Sun 10.30–3.45 (last entry)

♿ Good 💶 Free

HIGHLIGHTS

● Fin-de-Siècle and Old Masters Museums (▷ 30, 32–33)

● A stroll in the Parc de Bruxelles, with its tree-lined avenue and fountain

DID YOU KNOW?

● With the Brussels Card you get free entry to 40 museums and avoid the long lines to buy tickets. Valid for 24, 48 or 72 hours it comes with a guide, maps and discount offers. Buy it from tourist offices or online at visit.brussels.

This elegant neoclassical square is anchored by some powerful institutions: the Royal Palace, the Belgian Parliament and the Law Courts.

City views Famed for its symmetry and the uniformity of its architecture, the historic Place Royale has seen the coronation of Belgium's first king, Leopold I, and the funeral of King Leopold III. Presided over by a statue of Godefroy de Bouillon, a leader of the first crusade in the 11th century, and surrounded by some of the grandest buildings in Brussels, its location offers good views over the city.

Impressive buildings On the square's east side are the Église St-Jacques-sur-Coudenberg with its grand colonnaded portico and the imposing Law Courts, while the Musée Royaux de Beaux-Arts de Belgique (▷ 30, 32) dominates the west side. To the north is the Parc de Bruxelles, once the royal hunting grounds, laid out with statues and often used for concerts. The Palais de la Nation, on rue de la Loi, houses the Belgian Federal Parliament. Running south from the square, Rue de la Regence leads into Le Sablon district (▷ 35).

Royal Palace On the nearby Place de Palais, the Palais Royal is very much a working palace and the King's official residence, though the royals actually live at their Laeken palace (▷ 102). Every summer the palace opens some of its rooms to visitors and entry is free.

Browsing the weekend antiques market at Le Sablon

TOP 25

Le Sablon

The Sablon district, with its Grand and Petit Sablon squares, is the focus of the antiques trade. It is also perfect for a stroll, and its terraces are lovely places to sit and watch the world go by.

Place du Grand Sablon Many of Brussels' 17th-century aristocracy and bourgeoisie lived in this elegant square, which is now popular with antiques traders. The square has many specialist food shops, including Patisserie Wittamer (▷ 41), selling wonderful cakes, and chocolatier Pierre Marcolini (▷ 41).

Place du Petit Sablon Mayor Charles Buls commissioned this square in 1890. The statue of the Counts of Egmont and Horne, who were beheaded by the Duke of Alba during the wars of religion, was moved here from the Grand Place and is surrounded by statues of 16th-century scholars. Behind the garden, the 16th-century Palais d'Egmont, rebuilt in neo-classical style after a fire in 1891, is used for receptions by the Ministry of Foreign Affairs.

Église Notre Dame du Sablon The 15th-century church of Notre Dame du Sablon is a fine example of flamboyant Gothic architecture, built over an earlier chapel with a miraculous statue of the Virgin Mary. A hemp weaver from Antwerp heard celestial voices telling her to steal the Madonna statue at the church where she worshiped and take it to Brussels. The choir and stained-glass windows are beautiful.

CENTRAL BRUSSELS TOP 25

THE BASICS

* E6
* Church: 02 511 5741
* Church: Mon–Fri 9–6.30, Sat–Sun 9–7
* Restaurants, cafés
* 27, 95; tram 92, 93
* Good
* Antiques market Sat 9–5, Sun 9–2

HIGHLIGHTS

* Église Notre Dame du Sablon
* Statues on place du Petit Sablon
* Antiques market and shops
* Garden behind Palais d'Egmont
* Patisserie Wittamer (▷ 41)
* Pierre Marcolini chocolates (▷ 41)
* Gourmet food market, Thu 3–9pm

More to See

BOZAR

bozar.be

BOZAR, formally the Palais des Beaux Arts, was designed by Victor Horta in 1928. He left the art nouveau style of his earlier buildings behind and opted for a sterner Modernist construction. This is a lively venue for concerts and exhibitions of contemporary art. It also houses the Musée du Cinema.

🚇 E5–6 ✉ Rue Ravenstein 23 ☎ 02 507 8200 🚉 Parc/Park ♿ Good 🎫 Varies

CATHÉDRALE DES STS. MICHEL ET GUDULE

cathedralisbruxellensis.be

With its intriguing mixture of styles and influences, the cathedral of Sts. Michael and Gudule expresses Brussels' ability to compromise and is a fitting venue for state occasions. The earlier Romano-Gothic elements, particularly the ambulatory and choir, fit happily with those from the Late Gothic period. Restoration work exposed elements of an earlier Romanesque church (founded 1047), on which the cathedral was built.

🚇 E5 ✉ Parvis St.-Gudule ☎ 02 217 8345 🕐 Mon–Fri 7–6 (5 in winter), Sat 7.30–3.30, Sun 2–6 (5 in winter) 🚉 Gare Centrale/ Centraal Station ♿ Few 🎫 Inexpensive

CENTRALE

centrale.be

Brussels' first ever power plant, built in 1893, now houses CENTRALE for contemporary art. The large space hosts avant-garde art and organizes workshops for children.

🚇 D4 ✉ Place Ste.-Catherine 44 ☎ 02 279 6452 🕐 Wed–Sun 10.30–6 🚉 Ste.-Catherine/St.-Katelijne/Bourse 🎫 Moderate

ÉGLISE ST.-NICOLAS

Founded in the 12th century, this is one of the oldest churches in Brussels. Much rebuilt and restored, it houses many interesting works of art. A cannonball in the wall recalls the city's bombardment of 1695.

🚇 E5 ✉ Rue au Beurre 1 ☎ 02 513 8022 🕐 Mon–Fri 10–5.30, Sat–Sun 9–6 🚉 Bourse/Beurs 🚊 Tram 4, 32 🎫 Free

Henry Le Boeuf Concert Hall

The interior of the Cathédrale St.-Michel et Ste.-Gudule

LES MAROLLES

Dwarfed by the Palais de Justice and hemmed in by the elegant Sablon quarter, the Marolles is a reminder of working-class Brussels, with its narrow cobbled streets and plethora of vintage and bric-a-brac-shops. Rue Blaes and rue Haute are its main thoroughfares. Around place du Jeu de Balle are traditional cafés and on-trend shops. The flea market held here has unusual items at bargain prices, especially on Sunday mornings. As a fashionable crowd moves into the Marolles so ever more art galleries, clubs and cocktail bars open up and the organic (bio) market at rue Tanneurs 58 is a big attraction.

🔴 D7 ✉ Around place du Jeu de Balle 🚌 27, 48; tram 92, 93 ♿ Few ❓ Flea market daily 7–2; bio market Tue–Fri 11.30–6, Sat–Sun 10–4

MUSÉE BELVUE

belvue.be

This interesting museum reveals the history of Belgium since independence in 1830. It is housed in the Hôtel Bellevue, built in the late 18th century on the ruins of the 12th-century castle of the Dukes of Brabant, later Emperor Charles V's Coudenberg Palace. The museum gives access to the archaeological site of these impressive ruins.

🔴 E–F6 ✉ Place des Palais 7 ☎ 02 500 4554 🕐 Tue–Fri 9.30–5, Sat–Sun 10–6 🚇 Parc/Park 🚌 27, 38, 71, 95; tram 92, 93 ♿ Good 💰 Moderate

MUSÉE DE LA VILLE DE BRUXELLES

brusselscitymuseum.brussels

This 19th-century building, a careful reconstruction of the original Maison du Roi, is devoted to Brussels' history, and displays paintings, tapestries, maps and manuscripts, as well as changing temporary exhibitions.

🔴 E5 ✉ Grand Place ☎ 02 279 4350 🕐 Tue–Sun 10–5 🚇 Bourse/Beurs, Gare Centrale/Centraal Station ♿ Few 💰 Moderate; free 1st Sun of month

Displays at the Musée Belvue

MUSÉE RENÉ MAGRITTE

musee-magritte-museum.be

With the world's largest collection of works by the great Belgian surrealist, the René Magritte Museum spans three floors of the restored landmark building, Hôtel Altenloch. Starting from the top floor and working down, the displays follow the artist's themes and timeline.

🔢 E6 ✉ Place Royale 1 ☎ 02 508 3211 🕐 Mon–Fri 10–5, Sat–Sun 11–6 🚇 Gare Centrale/Centraal Station or Trône/Troon ♿ Good 💶 Expensive; free 1st Wed of month after 1pm

PALAIS DE JUSTICE

The Palais de Justice was one of King Leopold II's pet projects, designed by Joseph Poelaert in grand eclectic style to house Belgium's supreme court of law. The interior is overwhelming and there are grand views over Brussels from the terrace.

🔢 D–E7 ✉ Place Poelaert ☎ 02 508 6578 🕐 Mon–Fri 8–5. Closed holidays 🚇 Louise/ Louiza 🚊 Tram 92, 94 ♿ Good 💶 Free

ST.-GÉRY AND STE.-CATHERINE

Brussels was founded on the place St.-Géry in 979, when Charles, Duke of Lorraine, built a castle here. Now the square is a fashionable place. Rue Antoine Dansaert has stylish shops and rue des Chartreuses and chaussée de Flandres have great bars and restaurants.

🔢 D4–5 ✉ Around the rue Antoine Dansaert and place St.-Géry 🚇 Bourse/ Beurs, Ste.-Catherine/St.-Katelijne ♿ Good

THÉÂTRE ROYAL DE LA MONNAIE

lamonnaie.be

The first public theater for opera and ballet was built here in 1700. Napoleon rebuilt it in 1819 and to this day it is one of Europe's most beautiful opera houses. Behind the neoclassical facade lies an impressive grand foyer, sweeping staircase and a painted cupola.

🔢 E4–5 ✉ Place Royale 1 de la Monnaie ☎ 02 229 1200 🕐 Mon–Fri 10–5, Sat–Sun 11–6 🚇 De Brouckère ♿ Very good ❓ Tours available

Relaxing in a bar in St.-Géry

From Manneken-Pis to Jeanneke-Pis

This walk explores the historical heart of Brussels, with the Grand Place and the now-trendy area of St.-Géry, where the city was born.

DISTANCE: 1.5km (1 mile) **ALLOW:** 1–2 hours

START ┈┈┈┈┈

GRAND PLACE ▷ 26–27
🚇 E5 🚊 Gare Centrale or Bourse

① Leave the Grand Place (▷ 26) via rue Charles Buls. Walk along rue de l'Etuve, leading to Manneken-Pis (▷ 29).

② Turn right onto rue Grands-Carmes to rue du Marché au Charbon. Walk past Église Notre-Dame du Bon-Secours to boulevard Anspach.

③ Turn right onto the boulevard and then left onto rue des Riches Claires, with its 17th-century church. Turn right onto rue de la Grande Île.

④ Immediately left, a passageway leads to the back of the church and the original site of the River Senne. Return to place St.-Géry.

END

RUE DES BOUCHERS
🚇 E5 🚊 Gare Centrale or Bourse

⑧ Take a right onto rue des Fripiers and left onto rue Grétry, which becomes rue des Bouchers, where Jeanneke-Pis is signposted.

⑦ This leads to place Ste.-Catherine, built on the basin of Brussels' old port. Walk past the Tour Noire, part of the first city wall, back to boulevard Anspach, and cross over onto rue de l'Évêque to place de la Monnaie, with the Théâtre Royal de la Monnaie.

⑥ Walk along rue du Pont de la Carpe and then left onto rue Antoine Dansaert, where there are restaurants and trendy clothes shops. Take a right onto rue du Vieux Marché aux Grains.

⑤ A plaque on Halles St.-Géry shows the site of Brussels' origins.

Shopping

AKASO
akaso.eu
Combining Belgian design with Ethiopian influences, Akaso offers high quality, ethical and sustainable clothing and accessories for men and women.
🔲 E5 ✉ Galerie du Roi 1, Galeries Royale St.-Hubert ☎ 02 513 2007 🕐 Mon–Sat 10.30–6.30, Sun 2.30–5.30 🚇 Gare Centrale/Centraal Station

A. M. SWEET
Tea salon and shop with beautiful chocolates, crystallized flowers, *pain d'épices* and coffees.
🔲 D5 ✉ Rue des Chartreux 4 ☎ 02 513 5131 🕐 Tue–Thu 11–6.30, Fri 10.30–6.30, Sat 9.30–6.30 🚇 Bourse/Beurs

ANTICYCLONE DES AÇORES
anticyclonedesacores.be
A great travel bookstore with travel guides, maps, globes and travel literature in several languages.
🔲 D4 ✉ Rue Fossé aux Loups 34 ☎ 02 217 5246 🕐 Mon–Sat 10.30–6.30 🚇 De Brouckère

BELGE UNE FOIS
belgeunefois.com
Tap in to the Belgian sense of humor at this concept store in the Marolles district. From badges and sweatshirts to posters, mugs and tote bags, pick your favorite message for a fun souvenir.
🔲 D7 ✉ Rue Haute 89 ☎ 02 503 8541 🕐 Wed–Sat 11–6, Sun 1–6 🚊 27, 48

LA BOUTIQUE DE TINTIN
boutique.tintin.com
Tintin fans come here for everything from pyjamas, socks, cups, stationery, postcards and diaries to life-size statues of Tintin, Captain Haddock and Snowy and, of course, the books.
🔲 D5 ✉ Rue de la Colline 13 ☎ 02 514 5152 🕐 Mon 12–6, Tue–Sat 10–6, Sun 11–5 🚇 Gare Centrale/Centraal Station

CHRISTA RENIERS
christareniers.com
Beautiful contemporary silver and gold jewelry with a touch of Zen and no shortage of wit. Reniers' silver cufflinks and keyrings are fun, and the bracelets, rings and earrings have an elegance of their own.
🔲 E6 ✉ Rue Lebeau 61 ☎ 02 514 9154 🕐 Tue–Sat 12–6, Sun 1–5 🚊 27, 48, 95; tram 92, 93

DANDOY
maisondandoy.com
This bakery, founded in 1829, sells Brussels cookies such as *pain à la Grecque, speculoos* and *couque de Dinant* in all sizes and shapes, as well as Belgium's best marzipan. Once you are inside, this place is hard to resist!
🔲 E5 ✉ Rue au Beurre 31 (other branches at rue Charles Buls 14 and place St.-Job 22) ☎ 02 540 2702 🕐 Mon–Sat 9.30am–10.30pm, Sun 10.30–10 🚇 Bourse/Beurs 🚊 Tram 4, 32, 55, 56

FNAC
fnac.be
Brussel's largest bookstore, with titles in French, Dutch, English, German, Italian and Spanish, and a good music department.
🔲 E4 ✉ City 2, rue Neuve ☎ 02 275 1111 🕐 Mon–Thu, Sat 10–7, Fri 10–8 🚇 Rogier, De Brouckère 🚊 Tram 3, 4, 31, 32

GALERIES ROYALES ST.-HUBERT
grsh.be
Built in 1847 this was one of Europe's first grand shopping arcades. Here, under a soaring glass roof, elegant

shops sell stylish fashion, gifts and gourmet foods amid cafés, bars, even a cinema and theater.

🔢 E5 ✉ Galerie du Roi 5 🚇 Gare Centrale/Centraal Station

MAISON MARGIELA

maisonmargiela.com

Flagship store of the Paris fashion house founded by the cult Belgian designer Martin Margiela and now headed by John Galliano. His signature perfume "Mutiny" sums up the edgy style of the clothes and accessories that bear the Margiela name.

🔢 D4 ✉ Rue de Flandre 114 ☎ 02 223 7520 🕐 Mon–Sat 11–7 🚇 Bourse/Beurs, Ste.-Catherine/Ste.-Katelijne

MARY'S

mary.be

Chocolate connoisseurs shop here for hand-crafted pralines, truffles and marrons glacés made with only the finest ingredients and elegantly presented. The Mary story goes back to 1919 and members of the Belgian royal family are known to be fans. There is another store at 36 Galerie de la Reine.

🔢 E5 ✉ Grand Place 23 ☎ 02 514 9029 🕐 Daily 10–10 🚇 Gare Centrale/Centraal Station, Bourse/Beurs 🚋 Tram 92, 93

PATISSERIE WITTAMER

wittamer.com

This wonderful but expensive patisserie sells Brussels' best sorbets, chocolates and cakes that taste fab. At 6 Grand Sablon Square you can buy chocolates and macarons, at 12–13 place du Grand you can sit to enjoy the pastries.

🔢 E6 ✉ Place du Grand Sablon 6 and 12–13 ☎ 02 512 3742 🕐 Mon 1–6, Tue–Sat 10–7, Sun 10.30–6.30 🚋 Tram 92, 93

PIERRE MARCOLINI

eu.marcolini.com

Marcolini is winner of the Chocolatier of the World award, and his chocolate creations are some of the best, and most expensive, in Belgium. There are additional stores at 75 avenue Louise, Galerie de la Reine and 1302 chaussée de Waterloo.

🔢 F6 ✉ Rue des Minimes 1 ☎ 02 514 1206 🕐 Sun–Wed 10–7, Thu–Sat 10–7.30 🚌 48, 95; tram 92, 93

PLAIZIER

avecplaizier.be

A bright, fun and quirky shop selling a huge selection of retro postcards, posters and books. You can also pick up amusing and interesting gifts.

🔢 E5 ✉ Rue des Éperonniers 50 ☎ 02 513 9929 🕐 Mon–Sat 12–6 🚇 Gare Centrale/Centraal Station

LES SAGAS

lessagas.be

Everything in this beguiling shop tells of tradition and craftsmanship and comes with a story. It's great for unusual gifts for the home and family.

🔢 E5 ✉ Galerie Bortier 11, rue St.-Jean 17–19 ☎ 02 540 8906 🕐 Tue–Sat 11–6.30 🚇 Gare Centrale/Centraal Station

STIJL

stijl.be

In her temple of Belgian fashion, Sonja Noël stocks designers like Dries Van Noten, Sophie d'Hoore and Ann Demeulemeester. Kat en Muis, her shop for kids, and Stijl Men are nearby on place Nouveau Marché aux Grains.

🔢 D4 ✉ Rue Antoine Dansaert 74 ☎ 02 512 0313 🕐 Mon–Sat 10.30–6.30 🚇 Bourse/Beurs, Ste.-Catherine/St. Katelijne 🚋 Tram 3, 4, 31, 32

Entertainment and Nightlife

A LA MORT SUBITE

alamortsubite.com

This traditional bar was one of singer Jacques Brel's preferred watering holes. It even has its own brew, called *Mort Subite* (Sudden Death) because of its higher alcohol content.

⊞ E5 ⊠ Rue Montagne aux Herbes Potagères 7 ☎ 02 513 1318 ⏰ Mon–Sat 11am–1am, Sun 12–12 🚇 Gare Centrale/Centraal station

ANCIENNE BELGIQUE

abconcerts.be

The famous AB has been everything from 15th-century merchants' hall and bank vault to 20th-century music hall and is now one of Brussels' best pop and rock venues.

⊞ D5 ⊠ Boulevard Anspach 110 ☎ 02 548 2484 🚇 Bourse/Beurs

L'ARCHIDUC

archiduc.net

Funky art deco lounge and cocktail bar famed for live music, blues and swing. In the autumn and winter months, drop by for "Jazz After Shopping" on Saturday or "Round About Five" on Sunday, both from 5–7pm.

⊞ D5 ⊠ Rue Antoine Dansaert 6 ☎ 02 512 0652 ⏰ Daily 4pm–5am 🚇 Bourse/Beurs

BEURSSCHOUWBURG

beursschouwburg.be

A platform for young and innovative artists that offers performance art, movies and concerts with the accent on experimental.

⊞ D5 ⊠ Rue Auguste Orts 20–28 ☎ 02 550 0350 🚇 Bourse/Beurs 🚋 Tram 3, 4, 32

LE BOTANIQUE

botanique.be

The botanical gardens are now a cultural complex for the French-speaking community. There are concerts in the Orangerie, exhibitions in the Museum and plays in the Witloof Bar.

⊞ F4 ⊠ Rue Royale 236 ☎ 02 218 3732 🚇 Botanique/Botaniek 🚋 4, 61; tram 92, 93

BOZAR

bozar.be

This art nouveau complex (▷ 36) is Brussels' most prestigious concert venue. It is home to the Orchestre National de Belgique and its two halls, with perfect acoustics, provide the setting for a wide-ranging repertoire with visiting orchestras, choirs and soloists. Most of the city's big concerts take place here.

⊞ E5–6 ⊠ Rue Ravenstein 23 ☎ Box office: 02 507 8200 ⏰ Box office: Mon–Sat 9–7 🚇 Parc/Park or Gare Centrale/Centraal Station

CAFÉ CENTRAL

lecafecentral.com

A small but great venue where the music tends towards electro-rock and there are concerts and nightly DJ sets with late-night dancing Thursday–Saturday. Sunday night is movie night.

⊞ D5 ⊠ Rue de Borgval 14 ⏰ Daily 3pm–4am 🚇 Bourse/Beurs

CINEMATEK FILMMUSEUM

cinematek.be

This is the place to see the old cinema classics, as well as more recent movies and little-known jewels from around the world. Besides the permanent

TICKETS

Tickets for most big events in Brussels can be booked through the tourist office on the Grand Place (☎ 02 513 8940; visit.brussels) or FNAC in City 2, rue Neuve (☎ 02 275 1111, fnactickets.com, fees apply).

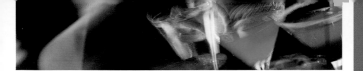

exhibition, five films are shown daily. Two are silent movies accompanied by piano music.

🚹 E5–6 ✉ Rue Baron Horta 9 ☎ 02 551 1900 🕐 Daily 5.30–10.30 🚇 Gare Centrale/Centraal Station 🚋 Tram 92, 93

CONSERVATOIRE ROYAL DE MUSIQUE

conservatoire.be

A perfect venue for classical and contemporary music concerts.

🚹 E6 ✉ Rue de la Régence 30 ☎ 02 511 0427 🚇 Louise/Louiza

LE FUSE

fuse.be

Popular Saturday night venue in a converted cinema, Le Fuse is one of Belgium's top techno music dance clubs where things hot up from the early hours.

🚹 D7 ✉ Rue Blaesstraat 208 ☎ 02 511 9789 🕐 Sat–Sun 11pm–7am 🚇 Porte de Hal/Hallepoort 🚋 3, 4, 51

HALLES DE SCHAERBEEK

halles.be

This superb 19th-century covered market is now a major cultural venue for the French-speaking community, with regular music, dance and drama.

🚹 G3 ✉ Rue Royal Ste.-Marie 22b ☎ 02 218 2107 🚇 Botanique/Botaniek

KAAITHEATER

kaaitheater.be

A jewel of 1930s architecture, this former cinema houses the Flemish Theater Institute. There are performances by influential Belgian dancers. The in-house Kaaicafé opens before and after performances.

🚹 D3 ✉ Square Sainctelette 20 ☎ 02 201 5959 🚇 Yser/Ilzer

MUSIC VILLAGE

themusicvillage.com

Lively jazz café with concerts, from the traditional to the most experimental, as well as shows featuring world music such as flamenco.

🚹 D5 ✉ Rue des Pierres 50 ☎ 02 513 5052 🕐 Dinner from 7pm, concerts from 8.30pm 🚇 De Brouckère, Bourse/Beurs

THÉÂTRE 140

le140.be

Good venue for international performances of dance, drama, music and English-language stand-up comedy.

🚹 J4 ✉ Avenue Eugène Plasky 140 ☎ 02 733 9708 🚋 Tram 7, 25

THÉÂTRE NATIONAL DE LA COMMUNAUTÉ FRANÇAISE

theatrenational.be

Most plays are in French, with a few English-speaking touring companies. The theater often arranges co-productions with Strasbourg.

🚹 E4 ✉ Boulevard Émile Jacqmain 111–115 ☎ 02 203 5303 🕐 Box office Mon–Fri 10–6, Sat 1–6 🚇 Rogier, De Brouckère 🚋 Tram 25, 51, 55

THÉÂTRE ROYAL DE LA MONNAIE

See page 38.

See page 38.

LGBTQ

Brussels is one of the most progressive cities in Europe. There is a concentration of bars, clubs and shops around rue du Marché au Charbon (D5) where people of all persuasions mix happily. A major center for information about the Brussels LGBTQ scene is the Rainbowhouse Bar, rainbowhouse.be, rue du Marché au Charbon 42, ☎ 02 503 5990. Also try patroc.com/gay/brussels.

Where to Eat

BELGA QUEEN (€€)

belgaqueen.be

An excellent brasserie, the Belga Queen
has it all—a wonderful oyster bar with
an almost endless choice, a beer bar
and a cigar lounge, all set in a lofty former bank with a huge stained-glass
skylight. As the name says, everything is
very Belgian, from the architecture to
the refined contemporary food.

🔡 D4 ⊠ Rue Fossé aux Loups 32 ☎ 02 217
2187 🕙 Mon–Thu 12–2.30, 6.30–11, Fri–Sat
12–2.30, 6.30–12 🚇 De Brouckère 🚊 Tram
3, 4, 31, 32

LA BELLE MARAÎCHÈRE
(€€–€€€)

labellemaraichere.com

This pleasant restaurant has the
ambience of a country house dining
room and offers excellent fish dishes.
Lobster soup with Armagnac and various
preparations of turbot are only some of
the possibilities, while even the starters
are a delight.

🔡 D4 ⊠ Place Ste.-Catherine 11 ☎ 02
512 9759 🕙 Fri–Tue lunch, dinner 🚇 Ste.-
Catherine/St.-Katelijne 🚊 Tram 3, 4, 31, 32

BOCCONI (€€€)

At the best Italian restaurant in town
you'll find stylish decor, excellent and
innovative Italian dishes and attentive
but relaxed service.

🔡 E5 ⊠ Hotel Amigo, rue de l'Amigo 1
☎ 02 547 4715 🕙 Lunch, dinner 🚇 Gare
Centrale/Centraal station, Bourse/Beurs

BONSOIR CLARA (€€–€€€)

bonsoirclara.net

This fashionable brasserie-style eaterie is
in a fashionable street, with a vibrant
setting. Come here to enjoy excellent
Mediterranean food with a few upscaled
favorites like hamburger and steak
featured too.

🔡 D5 ⊠ Rue Antoine Dansaert 22 ☎ 02
502 0990 🕙 Mon–Fri lunch, dinner; Sat–Sun
dinner 🚇 Bourse/Beurs

LE CERCLE DES VOYAGEURS (€€)

lecercledesvoyageurs.com

Grand café with leather armchairs and
a colonial atmosphere. The menu
includes dishes from around the world
and the wine list is also global.

🔡 D5 ⊠ Rue des Grands Carmes 18
☎ 02 514 3949 🕙 Daily 11am–midnight
🚇 De Brouckère

COMME CHEZ SOI (€€€)

commechezsoi.be

The famed chef, Pierre Wynants, has
retired from his signature restaurant,
but Comme Chez Soi's Michelin-starred
cuisine is now in the capable and creative hands of his daughter, Laurence,
and her chef husband, Lionel Rigolet.
Located in an elegant art nouveau townhouse, you need to reserve a table
weeks ahead to be able to enjoy the
haute cuisine on offer.

🔡 D6 ⊠ Place Rouppe 23 ☎ 02 512
2921 🕙 Tue–Wed 7–9, Thu–Sat 12–1.30, 7–9
🚇 Anneessens

COMOCOMO (€€)

comotapas.com

A Basque tapas bar is unusual here and this restaurant takes it one step further with the dishes going around on a sushi conveyor belt. The style is ultra contemporary and the food, including wild boar carpaccio, fried garlicky mushrooms and quail egg and bacon, is really good.

🔡 D5 ⊠ Rue Antoine Dansaert 19 ☎ 02 503 0330 🕐 Mon–Tue 6.30–10.30, Wed–Sun 12–2.30, 6.30–10.30 🚇 Bourse/Beurs

DARINGMAN (€)

Old-fashioned brown café turned hotspot, where the old locals meet the fashionable crowd.

🔡 D5 ⊠ Rue de Flandre 37 ☎ 02 512 4323 🕐 Tue–Thu noon–2am, Fri–Sat noon–3am, Sun noon–8pm 🚇 Ste.-Catherine/St.-Katelijne

DIVINO (€–€€)

divinoresto.be

A straightforward but very popular Italian restaurant with huge wood-oven baked pizzas and home-made pastas.

🔡 D5 ⊠ Rue des Chartreux 56 ☎ 02 503 3909 🕐 Tue–Fri lunch, dinner; Sat–Sun dinner 🚇 Bourse/Beurs

LE FALSTAFF (€–€€)

lefalstaff.be

At some time during an evening out everyone usually ends up at this huge but always busy art deco café with a vast terrace, heated in winter.

🔡 D5 ⊠ Rue Henri Maus 19 ☎ 02 511 8789 🕐 Daily 10am–midnight 🚇 Bourse/Beurs 🚊 Tram 4, 32, 55, 56

LA KASBAH (€–€€)

lakasbahresto.be

In a delightful dark-blue cave setting, this popular Moroccan restaurant delivers with its large menu of tajines, couscous and grills accompanied by Arabic music. There is also a good range of vegetarian and vegan options.

🔡 D5 ⊠ Rue Antoine Dansaert 20 ☎ 02 502 4026 🕐 Daily 12–2, 6.30–10 🚇 Bourse/Beurs 🚊 Tram 3, 4, 31, 32

LITTLE ASIA (€–€€)

littleasia.be

Popular, contemporary restaurant serving excellent Vietnamese, Thai and Chinese dishes, including vegetarian options.

🔡 D4 ⊠ Rue Ste.-Catherine 8 ☎ 02 502 8836 🕐 Wed–Sat 12–2, 6.30–10 🚇 Bourse/Beurs 🚊 Tram 3, 4, 31, 32

LA MANUFACTURE (€€)

lamanufacture.be

This restaurant, in the old Delvaux leather factory, serves delicious, inventive European food with a touch of Asia. You can sit outside in summer.

🔡 C–D5 ⊠ Rue Notre-Dame du Sommeil 12 ☎ 02 502 2525 🕐 Mon–Fri lunch, dinner; Sat dinner 🚇 Bourse/Beurs 🚊 Tram 3, 4, 31, 32

LA MER DU NORD (€)

noordzeemerdunord.be

Crowds flock to this popular fishmonger street stall for the seared scallops, salt

101 RESTAURANTS

Rue Antoine Dansaert has its fair share of eateries, as does rue des Chartreux, but Brussels' diners head for nearby rue de Flandre. This street is packed with eating possibilities, from the very Belgian and excellent Viva M'Boma (▷ 46) and Le Pré Salé at No. 20, modern French at SAN Bruxelles at No. 19 and fine dining at Gram at No. 86. Henri at Nos. 113–115 is a simple restaurant with fusion cuisine or you can discover Indian Ocean island dishes at Madagasikara at No. 10.

'n' pepper calamari, tuna fillet and oysters shucked to order. Expect a long wait at lunchtime, and you'll have to stand at a table to eat, but it's worth it.
🏁 D4 ⌧ Rue Ste.-Catherine 45 ☎ 02 513 1192 🕐 Tue–Sun 11–6 🚇 Ste.-Catherine/St.-Katelijne

LE PAIN QUOTIDIEN (€)

lepainquotidien.com

In this chain of tearooms, breakfast, lunch, snacks and afternoon tea are served around one big table. Try the breads, croissants, pastries and jams.
🏁 E6 ⌧ Rue des Sablons 11 ☎ 02 513 5154 🕐 Daily 7.30–7 🚌 33, 95; tram 92, 93
🏁 D5 ⌧ Rue Antoine Dansaert 16 ☎ 02 502 2361

SEA GRILL (€€€)

seagrill.be

Top chef Yves Mattagne creates high art on the plate with his superb fish dishes, whose dressings and sauces do not overwhelm the main component and are a culinary joy in their own right. This elegant restaurant has two Michelin stars, so reserve well in advance for a special occasion. The lunch menu represents good value.
🏁 E4 ⌧ Rue Fosse aux Loups 47 ☎ 02 212 0800 🕐 Mon–Fri lunch, dinner. Sat dinner 5- or 7-course menus only. Check the website for dates when closed 🚇 De Brouckère
🚌 Tram 3, 4, 31, 32

TAVERNE DU PASSAGE (€€)

taverne-du-passage.be

For old-time art deco Brussels, all polished wood, white tablecloths and sparkling glass, this long-established brasserie is the place to indulge in tradition. The menu has all the Belgian and French classics you'd expect, including shrimp croquettes and terrines, *choucroute* and *coquilles St.-Jacques*, mussels, veal and steaks, together with an excellent wine list.
🏁 E5 ⌧ Galerie de la Reine 30 ☎ 02 512 3731 🕐 Tue–Sun noon–11.30pm 🚇 Gare Centrale/Centraal Station 🚌 29, 38, 63, 71

VINCENT (€€–€€€€)

restaurantvincent.be

A real monument of Brussels cuisine, this is one of the most reliable restaurants in the area. Hunks of meat hang in the window. The dining room has hand-painted, marine-themed tiles and lots of character. Waiters expertly prepare dishes like steak flambée or steak tartare while you watch.
🏁 E5 ⌧ Rue des Dominicains 8–10 ☎ 02 511 2607 🕐 Wed–Mon 12–3, 6.30–11; closed 1–11 Jan and first two weeks in Aug 🚇 De Brouckère, Gare Centrale/Centraal Station

VISMET (€€€)

levismet.be

Vismet is superb fish restaurant with an open kitchen, a plain wood and white-tablecloth decor. As well as the delicious fish and seafood there are good steak dishes for meat-eaters.
🏁 D4 ⌧ Place Ste.-Catherine 23 ☎ 02 218 8545 🕐 Tue–Sat 12–2.30, 7–10 🚇 Ste.-Catherine/St.-Katelijne

VIVA M'BOMA (€€€)

vivamboma.be

"Long Live My Grandma" is an absolutely delightful restaurant in an old butcher's shop, with several awards in its pocket. It is a modest place, but the food is consistently excellent. The menu has many Belgian dishes, focusing on meat and offal.
🏁 D4 ⌧ Rue de Flandre 17 ☎ 02 512 15 93 🕐 Mon, Tue, Thu–Sat 12–2.30, 7–10.30 🚇 Ste.-Catherine/St.-Katelijne

South Brussels

South of the inner ring road is a newer Brussels, with the more residential areas of Ixelles and St.-Gilles. In recent years these districts have undergone a revival, with a wealth of new shops and restaurants.

Top 25

4

5

6
Slachthuizen en
Markten van
Kuregem
Erasmus
Hogeschool
Brussel
Albert
Clemenceau
Fiennes
RUE DE
FIENNESSTRAAT
N D Immaculée
Bodeghem
Bodegém
Musée de la
Gueuze
Lemonnier
RUE V LINTSTRAAT
Conseil /
Raad
Bara
BOULEVARD

7
Ecole
Technique
François-
Xavier
GARE
DU MIDI
ZUIDSTATION
Marché
du Midi
Gare du Midi /
Zuidstation
Suède
Zweden
Louise
de Louiza
Louise
Louiza
Stéphanie
Stefania

8
✠
Lerne Zenne
RUE DES DEUX GARES
TWEESTATIONS
Avenue du Roi /
Koningslaan
Bethléem
Bethlehem
ST
GILLIS
Guillaume Tell /
Willem Tell
Porte de Hal
Halleport
Musée d Folk
Parvis de
Saint-Gilles /
Sint-Gillis-
Voorplein
Parc
Jacques
Franck
Saint
Bernard
Hôtel des
Monnaies
Munthof
Faider

9
Orban
Saint Antoine
Saint Antonius
Wiels
AVENUE W CEUPPENSLAAN
Wiels
Wiels
Berthelot
Rochefort
Sainte Alène
Combaz
Barrière /
Barreel
Horta
Mais
Comm
Lombardie /
Lombardije
ST
GILLES
Moris
Janson
Janson
Trinité /
Drievuldigheid
Eglise
Sainte Trinité
Musée Horta
(Hortamuseum)
Ma Campagne

10
Sainte
Marie
Parc Duden
Dudenpark
Jupiter
Parc de Forest
Park van Vorst
Albert
Prison de
Saint Gilles
Gevangenis
Prison de Forest
Gevangenis van
Vorst
Darwin
Hôtel
Hannon
ELSENE

11
L'Union Saint Gilloise
Joseph Marien
FOREST VORST
Altitude Cent
Hoogte
Honderd
Saint Augustin
Berkendael
Berkendaal
Hôpital de
Saint Gilles
MOLIÈRE
Molière
N D
Annonciation
Institute Nat
du Sang
MOLIÈRELAAN
Institute Médical
Ed Cavell
Vanderkindere
Cavell
CHURCHILL
Churchill
Parc
Montj

12
H Hart
Sacré Coeur
Churchill
Parc
Brugmann
park
Musée David
et Alice van
Buuren
UKKEL

0 ————— 500 m
0 ————— 500 yds

A   **B**   **C**   **D**   **E**

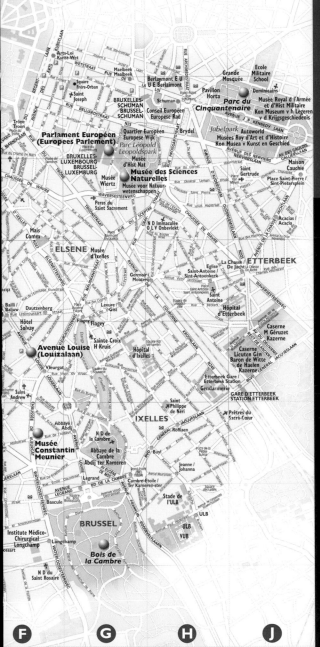

South Brussels

Arts-Loi
Kunst-Wet

Square
Frère-Orban

Saint
Joseph

Maelbeek E U
Berlaymont E U
La U E Berlaimont

BRUXELLES-
SCHUMAN
BRUSSEL-
SCHUMAN

Conseil Européen
Europese Rad

Grande
Mosquée

Pavillon
Horta

Ecole
Militaire
School

Dominicains

Musée Royal d'l'Armée
et d'Hist Militaire
Kon Museum v h Legeren
v d Krijgsgeschiedenis

Parc du
Cinquantenaire

Parlament Européen
(Europees Parlement)

Quartier Européen
Europese Wijk

Musée
d'Hist Nat

Musée
Wiertz

Parc Léopold
Leopoldspark

Jubelpark

Musées Roy d'Art et d'Histoire
Kon Musea v Kunst en Geschied

Brydel

Maison
Cauchié

Musée des Sciences
Naturelles

Musée voor Natuur-
wetenschappen

Saint
Gertrude

Place Saint-Pierre /
Sint-Pieterstplein

Peres du
Saint Sacrement

N D Immaculée
O L V Onbevlekt

Acacias /
Acacia

Mais
Comm

ELSENE

Musée
d'Ixelles

La Chasse /
De Jacht

ETTERBEEK

Eglise
Saint-Antoine /
Sint-Antoonkerk

Germoir /
Mouterij

Baili /
Baljuw

Dautzenberg

Levure /
Gist

Hôtel
Solvay

Flager Flagey

Saint
Antoine

Hôpital
d'Etterbeek

Avenue Louise
(Louizalaan)

Sainte Croix
H Kruis

Hôpital
d'Ixelles

Caserne
M Géruzet
Kazerne

Vleurgat

Caserne
Licuten Gén
Baron de Witte
de Haelen
Kazerne

Saint
Andrew

Saint
Philippe
de Néri

Etterbeek Gare /
Etterbeek Station

Gendarmerie

GARE D'ETTERBEEK
STATION ETTERBEEK

IXELLES

Prêtres du
Sacré-Coeur

Abbaye
Abdij

N D de
la Cambre

Roffiaen

Musée
Constantin
Meunier

Abbaye de la
Cambre
Abdij ter Kameren

Buyl

Jeanne /
Johanna

Legrand

Cambre-Etoile /
Ter Kameren-ster

Bascule

Stade de
l'ULB

ULB

Institute Médico-
Chirurgical
Longchamp

Longchamp

BRUSSEL

ULB

VUB

N D du
Saint Rosaire

Bois de
la Cambre

F   G   H   J

Parc du Cinquantenaire

HIGHLIGHTS

● Treasure Room at the Art & History Museum
● Fountains and gardens
● Views over the city from the top of the triumphal arch

DID YOU KNOW?

● Maison Cauchie, at rue des Francs 5 (open first weekend each month 10–1, 2–5.30, cauchie.be), is the finest example of art nouveau architecture in Brussels. Paul Cauchie, who built the house in 1905, was a sgraffito artist.

Built to celebrate 50 years of Belgian independence, this park has all you would imagine in the way of grand buildings— even its own triumphal arch. It also has some surprises.

The most famous city park King Leopold II ordered the building of the Palais du Cinquantenaire, with two huge halls, to hold the National Exhibition of 1880. The monumental arch was built in 1905, with the two colonnades linking the pavilions added later.

Remarkable monuments Several features here recall important international fairs. An Arab-inspired building, which housed a panorama of Cairo in the 1880 fair, is now Brussels' Grand Mosque. The temple-like Pavilion

Clockwise from top left: Red Ferraris line up in front of the Arc du Cinquantenaire; vintage cars at Autoworld; a shining exhibit at Autoworld; enjoying the Montgomery fountain in nearby avenue de Tervuren

THE BASICS

✚ H–J6

✉ Main entrances rue de la Loi and avenue du Chevalier

🚇 Merode, Schuman

🚌 22, 27, 80; tram 81, 82

Autoworld

autoworld.be

☎ 02 736 4165

🕐 10–5 (until 6 Sat–Sun)

🍴 Café

♿ Good

👊 Expensive

Musée Royal de l'Armée et d'Histoire Militaire

klm-mra.be

☎ 02 737 7811

🕐 Tue–Sun 9–5

🍴 Café

♿ Good   👊 Moderate

Art & History Museum

artandhistory.museum

☎ 02 741 7331

🕐 Tue–Fri 9.30–5, Sat–Sun 10–5

♿ Good

👊 Expensive

Horta-Lambeaux was erected in 1887, to designs by Victor Horta, to house the vast haut-relief of the *Human Passions* by Flemish sculptor Jef Lambeaux. It has very restricted opening hours.

Interesting museums One of the National Exhibition halls now showcases Autoworld, a prestigious collection of cars from 1886 to the present. The Musée Royal de l'Armée et d'Histoire Militaire incorporates an aviation museum, with planes displayed in a huge hangar, as well as housing weapons from medieval times to the present. The rich Art & History Museum, in the south wing of the Palais du Cinquantenaire, has items from ancient civilizations, Belgian archaeological discoveries and important European decorative arts.

Musée Horta

● Art nouveau originated in Britain in the 1880s, but Brussels architects Paul Hankar, Henri Van de Velde and especially Victor Horta made it completely their own style.
● ARAU offers excellent tours of art nouveau districts (☎ 02 219 3345; arau.org).
● A great way to see Brussels' art nouveau architecture is by bicycle (▷ 56, bicycle tour).
● A free brochure on art nouveau houses open to the public is available from the tourist office on the Grand Place.

Many of the grand buildings designed by architect Victor Horta have been destroyed, but here in his house, on the rue Américaine, the flowing lines and the play of light and space clarify his vision.

New style Victor Horta (1861–1947) built these two houses as his home and studio between 1898 and 1901. Now a museum and World Heritage Site, they illustrate the break he made from traditional townhouses, with their large, gloomy rooms. Horta's are spacious and airy, full of mirrors, white tiles and stained-glass windows. A light shaft in the middle of the house illuminates a banister so gracious and flowing that you just want to slide down it. The attention to detail is amazing, even down to the last door handle.

The stunning detailing in Musée Horta runs throughout the house

Art nouveau in St.-Gilles There are other interesting properties in residential St.-Gilles. Strolling around the area between rue Defacqz and St.-Gilles Prison, you can admire several examples of art nouveau style, dating from the late 19th to early 20th centuries. Paul Hankar designed the Ciamberlani and Janssens mansions at rue Defacqz 48 and 50, and his own house at No. 71. One of the most beautiful art nouveau facades in Brussels, designed by Albert Roosenboom, is at rue Faider 85. At rue de Livourne 83 you can see the private house of the architect Octave Van Rysselberghe, who also built the Otlet mansion at rue de Livourne 48. The Hannon mansion, built at avenue de la Jonction 1 by Jules Brunfaut, has an impressive fresco in the staircase. There are two more art nouveau houses at Nos. 12 and 14.

THE BASICS

hortamuseum.be

⊞ E9

✉ Rue Américaine, St.-Gilles 25

☎ 02 543 0490

🕐 Tue–Sun 2–5.30

🚌 54; tram 81, 92, 97 from place Louise

♿ Few

✋ Expensive

❓ Guidebooks and guided tours are available

More to See

AVENUE LOUISE

Avenue Louise is one of the places where you'll see *Bruxellois* heading for the designer boutiques. The avenue, and the high-end Ixelles district, are where bureaucrats come to spend their money; they crowd the many smart cafés, spilling onto the streets, and part with hundreds of euros in its stores. It is one of Brussels' main shopping areas, with boutiques, interior designers, showrooms, art galleries, hotels and restaurants.

➕ E–F–G7–10 ✉ Avenue Louise
🍴 Restaurants nearby 🚇 Louise/Louiza
🚌 2, 6, 33, 54; tram 8, 92, 93, 97 ♿ Good

BOIS DE LA CAMBRE

Once part of the Forest of Soignes, this green area was annexed by the city in 1862 and laid out in 1869 by landscape artist Edouard Keilig. Boating, bicycling, fishing and roller-skating are some of the activities.

➕ G11–G12 ✉ Main entrance on avenue Louise ⏰ Dawn–dusk 🚌 Tram 8, 93
♿ Few 🆓 Free

COLLÉGIALE DES STS. PIERRE ET GUIDON

The Romanesque crypt dates from the 11th century, but the superb Gothic church, with frescoes, is from the 14th to 16th centuries. The altar is illuminated by light filtering through the lovely stained-glass window above. The rare Celtic tombstone is believed to mark the grave of St.-Guidon.

➕ Off A7–A8 ✉ Place de la Vaillance
☎ 02 523 0220 ⏰ Daily 9–12, 2–5; services Mon–Thu 8.30, Fri 6pm, Sat 5.30, Sun 9.30, 11, 4.30. Closed during services 🚇 St.-Guidon/St.-Guido ♿ Few 🆓 Free

EUROPEAN PARLIAMENT

europarl.europa.eu

The brilliant Parlamentarium, the European Parliament's visitor center, is a great way to get to grips with how it all works. Interactive, informative and fun, with family activities and changing exhibitions.

➕ G6 ✉ Rue Wiertz 60 ☎ 02 283 2222
⏰ Mon 1–6, Tue–Fri 9–6, Sat–Sun 10–6
🚇 Schuman ♿ Good 🆓 Free

Striking architecture in the European Parliament district

MARCHÉ DU MIDI
The Marché du Midi is one of Europe's largest markets, with fruit and vegetables, fish, meat, clothes, pictures and household goods.
➕ C7 ✉ Near Gare du Midi 🕐 Sun 7am–1pm 🚇 Gare du Midi/Zuidstation 🚋 Tram 3, 4, 32, 51, 81, 82 ♿ Few 🎫 Free

MUSÉE CONSTANTIN MEUNIER
fine-arts-museum.be
Dedicated to the life and works of painter and sculptor Constantin Meunier (1831–1905), this museum was once his house and studio. Meunier was disturbed by the hard living conditions of the working class, and became famous for depicting suffering workers.
➕ F10 ✉ 59 rue de l'Abbaye ☎ 02 648 4449 🕐 Tue–Fri 10–12, 1–5 🚇 Louise/Louiza 🚋 Tram 93, 94 🎫 Free ♿ Difficult

MUSÉE DAVID ET ALICE VAN BUUREN
museumvanbuuren.be
This delightful museum is in the van Buurens' elegant art deco house. The interior and the gardens are stunning, and the art collection of the banker and his wife is equally remarkable with highlights including pieces by Brueghel and Van Gogh that shouldn't be missed.
➕ E12 ✉ Avenue Léo Errera 41 ☎ 02 343 4851 🕐 Wed–Mon 2–5.30 🚋 Tram 3, 4, 7 ♿ Few wheelchair facilities 🎫 Expensive

MUSEUM DES SCIENCES NATURELLES
brusselsmuseums.be
With the largest dinosaur gallery in Europe, home to the Bernissart Iguanodons, the Museum of Natural Sciences is a magnet for families. Five big exhibition spaces explore our world, from the earliest forms of life in the Gallery of Evolution to the human body in the Gallery of Humankind, through minerals, insects and urban species in BiodiverCITY.
➕ G7 ✉ Rue Vautier 29 ☎ 02 627 4211 🕐 Tue–Fri 9.30–5, Sat–Sun 10–6 🚇 Trône/Troon 🚋 34, 38, 80, 95 ♿ Moderate wheelchair access 🎫 Moderate

Museum des Sciences Naturelles

Art Nouveau Bicycling Tour

Brussels has a wealth of art nouveau architecture. This tour takes in works by two of the main players, Victor Horta and Paul Hankar.

DISTANCE: 4km (2.5 miles) **ALLOW:** 2 hours

START ⋯⋯

HÔTEL SOLVAY, AVENUE LOUISE
✚ F8–9 ⓜ Louise, then tram 94

END

PLACE LOUISE
✚ E7 ⓜ Louise

❶ Start at the fine Hôtel Solvay, built by Victor Horta in 1898. Cycle north-west along avenue Louise and take the third street to the left, rue Paul-Émile Janson. Here you'll see the Hôtel Tassel at No. 6, which was built by Horta in 1893.

❷ Turn right on rue Faider and then left onto rue Defacqz. No. 48 is a house by Paul Hankar, and No. 51 is his studio. Turn left on rue Simonis to place du Châtelain, with lots of cafés. Continue on rue du Page to rue Américaine and take a right to the Musée Horta (▷ 52–53).

❸ Continue along the street and take a left on chaussée de Charleroi. No. 55 is the remarkable art nouveau house Les Hiboux (the Owls) and next door is the superb Hôtel Hannon, which was built in 1903.

❹ From adjoining avenue de la Jonction take a right on rue Félix Delhasse, with two smaller art nouveau houses at Nos. 13–15. Go right on rue de la Glacière, left on chaussée de Waterloo and right onto avenue Ducpétiaux. Nos. 13, 15 and 47 are by Paul Hankar.

❽ Take a right onto rue Jourdan and continue to place Louise.

❼ Take a left on rue du Métal and then turn right on rue de l'Hôtel des Monnaies, with, at No. 66, Hôtel Winssinger, by Horta (1894).

❻ Turn right on rue Maurice Wilmotte and left on rue d'Irlande to place L. Morichar. Turn right on rue de Roumanie, left on rue de la Croix de St.-Pierre, with (Nos. 76, 78 and 80) more houses by Paul Hankar.

❺ There are art nouveau houses by lesser-known architects all along the way back. Take a left on rue du Portugal, then right on rue Moris, and left again on rue d'Espagne.

Shopping

ART DECO 1920–1940

artdecoannebastin.be

After admiring Brussels' amazing art deco and art nouveau façades, you may want to see some period furniture, and that is just what this shop specializes in.
⊞ D9 ✉ Avenue Adolphe Demeur 16, St.-Gilles ☎ 02 534 7025 🕐 Mon, Thu–Sat 11–6.30 🚊 Tram 3, 4, 51, 81, 83, 97

BEER MANIA

beermania.be

Here you'll find the largest selection of beers in town, with more than 400 types, from the most obvious to some rare ones. You can also buy correct glasses, sample beers in the back of the shop or attend classes or tasting sessions.
⊞ F7 ✉ Chaussée de Wavre 174–176 ☎ 02 512 1788 🕐 Mon–Sat (and Sun in Dec) 11–9 🚇 Porte de Namur/Naamsepoort

DE CONINCK

deconinckwine.com

Founded in 1886 in Waterloo, the firm is now in its fourth generation as a family business specializing in fine wines, primarily from France, where they have their own vignoble. The Ixelles branch is a trove of noble wines.
⊞ H12 ✉ Avenue du Pesage 1 ☎ 02 640 4465 🕐 Tue–Fri 11–2, 2.30–7, Sat 10.30–2, 2.30–7 🚊 Tram 8, 25

LES ENFANTS D'EDOUARD

lesenfantsdedouard.com

From Ralph Lauren and Gucci to Belgium's Olivier Strelli and Stella McCartney, this eclectic and delightfully eccentric shop deals in good condition, secondhand high fashion.
⊞ E8 ✉ Avenue Louise 175 ☎ 02 640 4245 🕐 Mon–Sat 10–6.30 🚇 Louise/Louiza 🚊 Tram 93, 94

HÔTEL DES VENTES VANDERKINDERE

vanderkindere.com

This expensive auction house specializes in art and objects from the 17th and 18th centuries.
⊞ D9 ✉ Chaussée d'Alsemberg 685–687, St.-Gilles ☎ 02 344 5446 🕐 Mon–Fri 9–12, 2–5. Phone for times of sale 🚊 Tram 51

HUNTING & COLLECTING

huntingandcollecting.com

This top fashion salon offers exciting clothing styles, also perfume, fashion media and cool ceramics. Lines include Givenchy, Kenzo and top Belgian designers such as Christian Wijnants.
⊞ D5 ✉ Rue des Chartreux 17 ☎ 02 512 7477 🕐 Tue–Sat 12–7, Mon 2–6 🚇 Bourse/Beurs 🚊 46; tram 3, 4, 31, 32

LIVING ROOM

A concept store that combines design with food, Living Room's open kitchen (good for weekend brunch) is surrounded by Scandinavian-style home furnishings, accessories and toys.
⊞ H6 ✉ Place Jean Rey 8 ☎ 02 231 1136 🕐 Mon–Fri 8–6, Sat–Sun 10–6 🚇 Maalbeck or Schuman 🚊 21, 27, 64

MATONGÉ

Matongé takes its name from an area in Kinshasha, in the Democratic Republic of Congo, a former Belgian colony, and it's one of the city's most exciting districts. At its heart is the Galerie Matongé, between chaussées Wavre and d'Ixelles. It sells African beauty products, foods, fashion and music. The pedestrian rue Longue Vie has several lively African bars and restaurants. At the split of the two *chaussées* is a wonderful giant mosaic by the Zairean artist Chéri Samba, worth the excursion.

LOOK 50

The oldest vintage store in Brussels has an excellent selection of secondhand clothes and accessories from the 1950s to 1980s. All are at very reasonable prices. In the same street are several other vintage stores, as well as other quaint little boutiques.

🔲 F7 ✉ Rue de la Paix 10 ☎ 02 512 2418
🕐 Mon–Sat 10.30–6.30 🚇 Porte de Namur/ Naamsepoort

MARCHÉ PLACE DU CHÂTELAIN

This delightful square has a good selection of restaurants and bars that are perfect for a lunch stop and is one of the liveliest people-watching spots in Brussels. On Wednesday afternoons, between 2pm and 7pm, food-lovers flock here for the city's best food market, with fine charcuterie, interesting cheeses, homemade jams, wines and delicious pastries.

🔲 E–F9 ✉ Place du Châtelain 🕐 Wed 2–7
🚋 Tram 81, 92

NATAN COUTURE

natan.be

The upscale fashions on display at this imposing mansion store change seasonally but tend to emphasize an elegant and subtle femininity. This outlet of Natan is one of a small chain in Belgium and close-by countries.

🔲 E8 ✉ Avenue Louise 158 ☎ 02 647 1001
🕐 Mon–Sat 10–6 🚋 Tram 93, 94

SENTEURS D'AILLEURS

senteursdailleurs.com

A sumptuous boutique with a selection of the perfumes, home fragrances and skincare items made by perfumers who don't cater to the mass market. Needless to say, the store smells divine and has a totally relaxing atmosphere. If the choice is too overwhelming, the staff are all experts who trained as "noses" and can assist in finding something that suits you to perfection.

🔲 F8 ✉ Place Stéphanie 1A (off avenue Louise) ☎ 02 511 6969 🕐 Mon–Sat 10–6.30
🚇 Louise/Louiza 🚋 Tram 94

LA SEPTIÈME TASSE

7etasse.com

Celebrating "the simple pleasures of tea" this little emporium, where you'll find teas and tisanes from around the world and tempting specialist mixes, is a treat for tea connoisseurs.

🔲 F9 ✉ Rue du Baillie 37 ☎ 02 647 1971
🕐 Tue–Sat 11–7 🚇 Louise/Louiza 🚋 54; tram 81, 93

SERNEELS

serneels.be

While this may not be the top spot for the latest TV tie-in toy, this spacious store is a wonderland of quality (and expensive) traditional and contemporary toys, from tiny ducklings to full-size cars and fine rocking horses. There is also a range of games and pastimes for older children.

🔲 E8 ✉ Avenue Louise 69 ☎ 02 538 3066
🕐 Mon–Sat 9.30–6.30 🚇 Louise/Louiza
🚋 Tram 94

QUARTIER DU CHÂTELAIN

The quiet streets and elegant art nouveau houses in this district attract a young crowd, and the area around place du Châtelain is a shopping hub. There is a picturesque food market on Wednesday afternoons on the square, and some great restaurants and interesting fashion boutiques in the streets adjoining the square, such as rue de l'Aqueduc, rue Simonis, rue du Page and rue Faider.

Entertainment and Nightlife

THE BLACK SHEEP

The Black Sheep has a good range of craft beers and gins plus a menu of well-prepared pub food, with DJs and live music at weekends. It's also home to stand-up English Comedy Brussels.
➕ G8 ✉ Chausée de Boondael 8 ☎ 02 644 3803 🕐 Wed, Thu, Sun 5pm–1am, Fri–Sat 5pm–3am 🚌 59; tram 81

CHEZ MOEDER LAMBIC

moederlambic.com
With some 400 Belgian beers to choose from, you're sure to find something to your taste in this jewel of Belgian bars. On warm summer evenings you can imbibe outside at a table on the street.
➕ D9 ✉ Rue de Savoie 68 ☎ 02 544 1699 🕐 Mon–Thu 4pm–2am, Fri 4pm–3am, Sat 10.30am–3am, Sun 10.30am–midnight 🚇 Lombardie 🚌 Tram 81, 97

FLAGEY

flagey.be
This is a wonderful arts venue in the old art deco-style state TV buildings. Shaped like a cruise liner, it stages performances of jazz, world, classical and contemporary music plus festivals and talks in a packed calendar of events. It also has Brussels' most comfortable cinemas showing a wide range of film genres.
➕ G8 ✉ Place Sainte-Croix, Ixelles ☎ 02 641 1010 🚌 38, 59, 60, 71; tram 81

FOREST NATIONAL

forest-national.be
The largest concert hall in Brussels, Forest National can hold over 8,000 spectators. It hosts big-name concerts as well as staging popular musicals, ballets, operas, extravaganzas on ice and sporting events.
➕ B12 ✉ Avenue Victor Rousseau 208 ☎ 02 400 6970 🚌 48, 54; tram 32, 82, 97

SOUNDS JAZZ CLUB

soundsjazzclub.be
This is a great jazz café that regularly features the best international and local jazz musicians. It's located near place Ferdinand Lecocq, which is stocked with good bars as well making for a complete night out.
➕ F7 ✉ Rue de la Tulipe 28, Ixelles ☎ 02 512 9250 🕐 Mon–Sat 8pm–4am 🚇 Porte de Namur/Naamsepoort 🚌 34, 38, 54, 71

LA SOUPAPE

In its homey nook close to les Étangs d'Ixelles, this small bar-theater puts on a steady diet of *chanson française* (mostly on Fridays and at the weekends), lovingly presented and performed.
➕ G9 ✉ Rue Alphonse de Witte 26a ☎ 02 649 5888 🚌 38, 59, 60, 71; tram 81

LE TAVERNIER

le-tavernier.be
This lively bar has a huge terrace area and indoor space, but it can often be hard to find a place to sit. Most of the regulars tend to hang out at the bar, or dance the early hours away to jazz or electro on weekends.
➕ G8-9 ✉ Chaussée de Boondael 445 ☎ 0475 241 523 🕐 Daily 11am–early morning 🚌 71, 95; tram 8, 25

THÉÂTRE DE POCHE

poche.be
Occupying a leafy site at the north end of the Bois de la Cambre, the "Pocket Theater" focuses on socially committed performance—though not to the extent of being unwilling to indulge in laughter—most of it in French.
➕ G11 ✉ Chemin de Gymnase 1a (reached from avenue Legrand) ☎ 02 649 1727 🚌 38; tram 7, 93, 94

Where to Eat

AU VIEUX BRUXELLES (€€)

auvieuxbruxelles.com

Founded in 1882, this place virtually
oozes old-fashioned *Bruxellois* charm
and quality. Diners pile in to sample its
trademark multifarious *moules* (mussels) specialties, along with the other
seafood and local dishes on the menu.
Polished wood paneling and classic red-
checked tablecloths set the tone inside.

➕ F7 ◻ Rue St.-Boniface 35 ☎ 02 503
3111 🕐 Sun–Thu 6.30–11.30, Fri–Sat 6.30–
midnight 🚇 Porte de Namur/ Naamsepoort
🚌 54, 71

AUX MILLE ET UNE NUITS (€€)

milleetunenuits.be

This Tunisian restaurant stands out in an
area packed with North-African eateries.
Inside, it is an interpretation of a tent in
the desert, with fairy lights replacing
the stars in the sky. The food, from the
salads and little pies to the couscous
with lamb and onions, is delicious.

➕ D8 ◻ Rue de Moscou 7 ☎ 02 537
4127 🕐 Tue–Sun 6.30–11 🚇 Porte de Hal/
Halleepoort 🚌 Tram 3, 4, 51

BRASSERIE VERSCHUEREN (€)

This archetypal Brussels brown café has
art deco touches and a great beer selection. It attracts lots of regulars from the
local community who clearly enjoy it's
relaxed and friendly atmosphere.

➕ D8 ◻ Parvis de St.-Gilles 11 ☎ 02 539
4068 🕐 Daily 11am–2am or later 🚌 Tram
3, 4, 51

CAFÉ BELGA (€)

Huge bar-restaurant in the old cruise-
liner-shape television building (▷ 59)
overlooking the lake in Ixelles. The large
terrace is a good place for breakfast, or
a drink before a movie, or you can
watch the passers-by.

➕ G8 ◻ Place Eugène Flagey 18 ☎ 02
640 3508 🕐 Open 24 hours 🚌 38, 60, 71;
tram 81

LE CHOU DE BRUXELLES €€

lechoudebruxelles.be

Serving Belgian specialities and famed
for offering 30 different ways of cooking
mussels, this friendly little restaurant, in
a quiet residential street off the Avenue
Louise, has Brussels' memorabilia on
the walls and umbrella-shaded tables
out on the terrace.

➕ E8 ◻ Place de Florence 26 ☎ 02 537
6995 🕐 Tue–Sat 12–2, 6.30–10 🚌 Tram
8, 93

LE CLAN DES BELGES (€€)

leclandesbelges.com

In this contemporary Belgian restaurant
you can sample the country's traditional
fare with an elegant modern twist. The
setting is hip and the prices moderate.

➕ F7 ◻ Rue de la Paix 20 ☎ 02 511
1121 🕐 Daily 12–2.30 (to 3 Sat–Sun), 7-11
🚇 Porte de Namur/ Naamsepoort 🚌 54, 71

LE FILS DE JULES (€€)

filsdejules.be

Popular Basque restaurant serving delicious cuisine from southwest France in a stylish setting. The wine list is good.
🚑 E9 ✉ 37 rue du Page ☎ 02 534 0057
🕐 Mon–Fri 7pm–11pm, Sat–Sun 7pm–midnight 🚋 54; tram 81

LE FRAMBOISIER DORÉ (€)

The most delicious sorbets in town, home-made in the traditional way, and with a wealth of tastes, including *speculoos*, the Belgian version of gingerbread.
🚑 F9 ✉ Rue du Bailli 35 ☎ 02 647 5144
🕐 Daily 1–9 🚋 54; tram 81, 83

L'HORLOGE DU SUD (€–€€)

horlogedusud.be

Lively West African brasserie with Congolese and Senegalese dishes, which include a lot of fish, yams and vegetables. Enjoy exotic cocktails with names such as "Sunny Mood." The weekday buffet lunch is good value.
🚑 F–G7 ✉ Rue du Trône 141 ☎ 02 512 1864 🕐 Mon–Fri 11–3, 6–midnight, Sat 6pm–midnight 🚇 Trône/Troon 🚋 34, 80

MAISON ANTOINE (€)

maisonantoine.be

Generally regarded as the best *frietkot* in Brussels, a stall with cones of delicious "Belgian" fries and a wide range of sauces and meaty accompaniments, which are allowed to be consumed in the cafés around the square.
🚑 H7 ✉ Place Jourdan ☎ 02 230 5456
🕐 Sun–Thu 11.30am–1am, Fri–Sat 11.30am–2am 🚇 Schuman 🚋 22, 34, 36

LA QUINCAILLERIE (€€€)

quincaillerie.be

An elegant and delightful restaurant in an old hardware store, a short walk from the Horta Museum (▷ 52). La Quincaillerie specializes in fish and seafood but you'll also find other delights in this restaurant with its own farm.
🚑 E9 ✉ Rue du Page 45 ☎ 02 533 9833
🕐 Mon–Fri lunch, dinner; Sat dinner only
🚋 54; tram 8, 81, 83

ROUGE TOMATE (€€€)

rougetomate.be

Classical elegance, balanced by contemporary design, complement the subtle and delicious food by an award-winning chef at this popular restaurant with a wooded terrace, garden and a cocktail bar overlooking Avenue Louise.
🚑 F8 ✉ Avenue Louise 190 ☎ 02 647 7044
🕐 Mon–Fri 12–2.30, 7–10.30, Sat 7–10.30
🚋 54; tram 8, 81, 93

L'ULTIME ATOME (€€)

ultimeatome.com

A brasserie that is both fashionable and traditional, with a large variety of beers and other drinks, simple but good Belgian dishes and long opening hours. Very popular on weekends, when locals come for breakfast and lunch. The terrace is a great spot for people watching.
🚑 F7 ✉ Rue St-Boniface 14 ☎ 02 513 4884 🕐 Mon–Fri 8am–12.30am, Fri–Sat 9am–1am, Sun 10am–12.30am 🚇 Porte de Namur/Naamsepoort 🚋 54, 71

VEGETARIAN CHOICE

Specifically vegetarian restaurants in Brussels include Les Nourritures Terrestres (✉ Parvis de Sainte-Gilles 43 ☎ 0498 595 334); Moonfood (✉ Rue des Colonies 58 02 303 4332); TICH Healthy Living Vegan store with café (✉ Rue de Namur 25 ☎ 02 503 8330); The Judgy Vegan (✉ Rue des Capucins 55 ☎ 02 540 8038).

Bruges

Bruges never fails to impress, with its romantic canals, quaint cobbled streets, medieval facades, bridges and towers and amazing collection of Flemish masters.

KOMVEST WALWEIN

St-Joz
kliniek

Sinte-Claradreef

ST-GILLIS

Kon-
Athene

Amunianter

Bidderss

Hoedermakersstr

Domini-
canessen

Ezelpoort

Elf Julistr

Blokstr

Biezenstr

Klaverstraat

KON. ELISABETHLAAN

VLAMINGDAM SINT-JORISSTRAAT

Anglikaansekerk

GULDEN · VLIESLAAN

Ezelstraat

H Losschaertstr

J Boninstr

Raamstr

Rozenstr

Karmelietenkerk

Poitevinstr

Augustijnenrei

Jezuïetenkerk

Woensda
markt

VLAMINGSTR

Jan va
Eyckpl

GULDEN
VLIESBRUG

Beenhouwersstraat

Groenestr

Zakske

Zak

Grauwwerkersstr

Oude Leeuwstr

St-Jakobskerk

Sint-Jakobsstr

Frietmuseum

Stadsschouwburg

St-Jan

Choco-
Story

st

Stadspark
Sebrechts

Stedelijk
Conservatorium

Naaldenstr

HOEFIJZERLAAN

Mortierstr

Brandstr

Paalstr

Lane

Guido Gezelle laan

Moerstraat

Muntplein

Wulf
hagestr

Noord: zandstraat

Geld muntstr

Zilverstr

Eiermarkt

Historium

Markt

Belfort
en Hallen

Steenstr

Woolstr

B

Pr
E

Oude Burg

Huiden:
vettersplein

Dijver

Buiten de
Smedenpoort

SMEDENSTR

Hendrik

Maagdenstr

Beurshalle

Hauwersstr

Conscience laan

KONING · TALBERT · I · LAAN

Zuidzandstr

Kathedraal
St-Salvador

Arentshuis

De Vesten
en Poorten

Kapucijnen

Sint-Godelieve-abdij

Boeverlestraat

Concert-
gebouw

St-Jan
Kunstcentrum

Bisschoppelijk Paleis

Arch
museum

Mariastr

Gruuthuse
Museum

Groeni
Museu

Onze-Lieve-
Vrouwekerk

St-Janshospitaal en
Memling Museum

Zonneke
Meers

Westmeers

Oostmeers

Begijnhof

Wijngaardstr

Diamantmuseum

Oli

Arsenaalstr

Katelijnestr

Boeverlepoort

Brouwerij de
Halve Maan

Wijngaard-
plein

Kliniek
Minnewater

Minnewater-
park

Minnewater

KATELIJNEBR

BUITEN · BEGIJNENVEST

footbridge

BUITEN KATELIJNEVEST

0   250 m
0   250 yds

I

2

3

4

a

b

Begijnhof

- The courtyard
- Statue of Our Lady of Spermalie
- *Béguine's* house

TIPS

- The courtyard is particularly beautiful in early spring, abloom with daffodils.
- Next to the Begijnhof is the equally picturesque Minnewater (▷ 85), the so-called Lovers' Lake, lined with trees.

A haven of tranquility, the fine enclosed courtyard of the Begijnhof is one of the oldest in Belgium, and one of Bruges' most picturesque corners.

Closed court From the 12th century onward, single or widowed pious women started living together in communities, often after losing their men to the Crusades. They took vows of obedience to God and spent their days praying and making lace for a living. Their cottages were built around a courtyard and surrounded by walls. There were many of these *Begijnhoven (Béguinages)*, but the one in Bruges is the best preserved. Since 1927, the Bruges Begijnhof has been occupied by Benedictine nuns, whose severe black-and-white habits are a reminder of those of the *béguines* who once lived there.

From left: A statue of Our Lady sits on the facade of the Begijnhof and spring flowers brighten the lawn

The church Several times a day the nuns walk to the church through the green garden at the side of the square. The simple church (1605) is dedicated to St. Elisabeth of Hungary, whose portrait hangs above the entrance. She also appears in a painting by Bruges master Lodewijk de Deyster (1656–1711). The most important work is the statue of Our Lady of Spermalie (c.1240). On the left wall as you face the altar is a superb statue of Our Lady of Good Will. The remarkable alabaster sculpture of the Lamentation of Christ at the High Altar dates from the early 17th century.

A *béguine's* **house** The tiny museum near the gate is a reconstruction of a 17th-century *béguine's* house, complete with furniture and household goods.

THE BASICS

➕ b4
✉ Wijngaardplein
☎ 050 33 00 11
🕐 Begijnhof daily 6.30–6.30; church 7–12.15, 3–6; museum Mon–Sat 9.30–12, 3–6, Sun 10.45–6
🚌 1, 11, 12
♿ Moderate
✋ Free. Museum inexpensive

Burg

HIGHLIGHTS

● Gotische Zaal in the
Stadhuis
● Stadhuis facade
● Mantelpiece of Charles V
in Brugse Vrije (Liberty of
Bruges) museum
● Basiliek van het
Heilig-Bloed (▷ 83)

TIP

● Admire the square at
night, when the crowds
have gone.

**This historic enclave evokes medieval
Bruges better than any other part of
the city. Its impressive buildings once
contained the offices of the church, city,
county and judicial authorities.**

A separate entity Until the 18th century, the
Burg was walled in and locked with four gates.
The north side of the square was dominated by
the 10th-century St. Donatian's Church, sold
by auction and torn down soon after in 1799.
(Some of its foundations can be seen in the
basement of the Crowne Plaza hotel.)

The square The whole of the square's west
side was once the Steen, an impressive 11th-
century tower; only the porch beside the stairs
to the Basiliek van het Heilig-Bloed (▷ 83)

Clockwise from top left: Bruges' Town Hall is the oldest in Belgium; visitors enjoy a horse-drawn carriage tour of the Burg; ornate carvings decorate the buildings surrounding the historic square

remains. To the southeast is the Flemish-Renaissance Civiele Griffie (Civil Recorders' House 1535–37). On the square's east side is the early 18th-century version of the Landhuis van het Brugse Vrije, the one-time seat of government of the Vrije, an autonomous rural and coastal region of the medieval period. Inside the palace is the *Mantelpiece of Charles V*, a Renaissance work of art by Lancelot Blondeel.

Stadhuis Built between 1376 and 1420, Bruges' town hall is the oldest in Belgium. Although its turreted sandstone facade dates from 1376, the statues on its Gothic facade date from the 1970s. The Gotische Zaal (Gothic Room) is where Duke Philip the Good called together the first States General of the Ancient Low Countries in 1464.

THE BASICS
✚ c3
✉ Burg
🕐 Town Hall (Gothic Room) daily 9.30–5. Museum: Brugse Vrije daily 9.30–5
🍴 Restaurants nearby
🚌 All buses to the Markt
♿ Very good
👆 Moderate
❓ Concerts in summer

Canal Cruise

Take a relaxing canal cruise within Bruges (left) or a longer trip to Damme (below)

THE BASICS

📧 Departure points:
Rozenhoedkaai,
Nieuwstraat,
Huidenvettersplein,
Wollestraat, Katelijnestraat
🕐 Generally March–Nov
10–6; also during the
Christmas period in mild
weather and some evening
cruises in summer
💶 Expensive

HIGHLIGHTS

● Groenerei
● Meebrug
● The smallest window in
Bruges at the Gruuthuse
Museum (▷ 74)
● Views of the Onze-Lieve-
Vrouwekerk (▷ 78)

TIPS

● Illuminated evening
tours, offered in summer,
are particularly pleasant.
● There is a flea market
along the Dijver on Sunday
in summer.
● For a longer canal trip,
take the boat to Damme
(▷ 96–97).

Bruges is often referred to as "the Venice of the North" and its *reien* (as the Brugeans call their canals) provide much of the city's romantic charm. Taking a boat on the canals is also one of the best ways to explore the heart of Bruges.

Where to start Several companies offer the same canal cruise that can be picked up from various departure points, including the Vismarkt (on Huidenvettersplein) and Dijver (on Nieuwstraat and Wollestraat). Commentary is given in several languages. There are regular departures throughout the day (see the side panel for when the boats run).

Highlights to spot The view of the Groenerei/ Steenhouwersdijk seen from the Vismarkt is one of the most idyllic scenes in Bruges. The Meebrug and the Peerdenbrug are two of the city's oldest stone bridges. At the end of Groenerei is the Godshuis (Almshouse) de Pelikaan. Rozenhoedkaai is another wonderful corner, with rear views of the buildings of the Burg and Huidenvettersplein and of the Duc de Bourgogne hotel. Along the Dijver are some of Bruges' grandest buildings, including the Gruuthuse Museum (▷ 74) and Onze-Lieve-Vrouwekerk (▷ 78). The canal becomes much more intimate after that and has several wooden medieval houses, before it ends at the Begijnhof (▷ 66), just before the Minnewater (▷ 85), which was the outer port of Bruges before the river silted up.

Find out what makes
Belgian chocolates
so special at the
Chocolate Museum

TOP
25

Choco-Story

Bruges is famous for its many chocolate shops, but this chocolate museum tells you all you ever needed to know about this delicious product, from the history of cocoa to the production of the famous Belgian pralines.

Chocolate history The museum is housed in the grand 15th-century Maison De Croon, an old wine tavern and later a pastry bakery. The first part of the museum evokes 2,500 years of chocolate history, through an impressive and well-explained collection of more than 1,000 objects illustrating the origins and evolution of chocolate. The earliest finds date from 600BC, when traces of cocoa were found in terracotta pots used by the Mayas of Colha (now in Belize, Central America), who were believed to drink their hot chocolate with a lot of foam. In 1519 the conquistadores discovered America and also the cocoa drink, which during the 17th and 18th centuries became increasingly popular with the European royals and aristocracy. Only much later was chocolate eaten as a confectionery bar.

Pralines and tastings The museum also explains how chocolate is made, with particular attention to the differences in ingredients and production processes over the years. At the end of the visit there is a demonstration of how the pralines are made. To round off the visit there is a tasting of the freshly made chocolates, and you can talk to the expert chocolate-maker.

THE BASICS

choco-story-brugge.be
✚ c2–3
✉ Wijnzakstraat 2
(St.-Jansplein)
☎ 050 61 22 37
🕐 Sep–Jun daily 10–5
(closed some days in Jan),
Jul–Aug 10–6
🚌 Any bus to the Markt
🎫 Moderate

HIGHLIGHTS

● *Chocolateros*, 19th-century ceramic vases with a pouring lip and a tube for blowing air into the chocolate to create foam
● Maison De Croon
● Chocolate tasting

BRUGES TOP 25

Groeninge Museum

Jan van Eyck's serene *Portrait of Margaretha van Eyck* and Gerard David's gruesome *Judgment of Cambyses,* portraying a magistrate being skinned alive, are so arresting that it is easy to overlook the contemporary art found in this impressive museum.

The Flemish Primitives The 15th-century Flemish Primitives were so named in the 19th century to express a desire to recapture the pre-Renaissance simplicity in art. Room 1 shows works by van Eyck (*c*.1390–1441), including the *Portrait of Margaretha van Eyck*, the painter's wife. There are two works by Hans Memling—the *Moreel Triptych* and two panels of *The Annunciation*—as well as works by Rogier van der Weyden and the last of the

Clockwise from far left: Visitors admiring the art on display in the Groeninge Museum; The Last Judgement; an oil painting by Jordaens

Flemish Primitives, Gerard David, including his *Judgment of Cambyses*. In Room 7, the 16th-century works of Pieter Pourbus illustrate the Italian influence on Flemish style. In Room 8, look for the lovely baroque *Portrait of a Bruegan Family* by Jacob van Oost (1601–71).

Modern Flemish masters Emile Claus (1849–1924) and Rik Wouters (1882–1916) are well represented. Also look for works by James Ensor, Gustave van de Woestijne and Rik Slabbinck; works by Constant Permeke represent the best of Flemish Expressionism. There are two paintings by Paul Delvaux and one by René Magritte. The last room shows works by Brugeans Luc Peire, Gilbert Swimberghe, and Roger Raveel and also contains a cabinet by avant-garde artist Marcel Broodthaers.

THE BASICS	
✚	c3
✉	Dijver 12
☎	050 44 87 11
🕐	Tue–Sun 9.30–5
🍴	Cafeteria
🚌	1, 11
♿	Good
💰	Expensive

Gruuthuse Museum

The museum's eye-catching emblem outside, and porcelain and tapestries inside

THE BASICS

- ✚ b3
- ⊠ Dijver 17
- ☎ 050 44 87 43
- 🕐 Tue–Sun 9.30–5
- 🚌 1, 2, 4, 6, 11–16
- ♿ Phone for information
- 💷 Expensive; Brangwyn Museum moderate

HIGHLIGHTS

- ● Sculpture rooms
- ● Prayer balcony
- ● Gombault and Macée Tapestry series
- ● Illuminated courtyard at night
- ● Smallest window in Bruges, seen from the Boniface Bridge
- ● Views from loggia over Reie, Boniface Bridge and Onze-Lieve-Vrouwekerk

The facade and peaceful courtyard of the Gruuthuse Palace take you back to medieval times. It is a delight to stroll around the nearby Arentspark and watch boats glide under the Boniface Bridge, one of Bruges' most romantic corners.

The palace of Gruuthuse Built in the late 15th century by the humanist and arts lover Lodewijk van Gruuthuse, this medieval palace now houses the Gruuthuse Museum, a fascinating collection of antiques and applied arts, which has recently undergone a major restoration. There are some fine sculptures, including an early 16th-century Gothic kneeling angel rendered in oak; the impressive *Christ, Man of Sorrows* (c.1500); and the 15th-century *Reading Madonna* by Adriaan van Wezel.

Brugean tapestries Well-preserved 17th-century examples in the Tapestry Room represent the *Seven Liberal Arts*; and some fine baroque wool and silk counterparts have pastoral themes, including the excellent comic-strip-like tapestry the *Country Meal*. The prayer room (chapel) is in the form of a balcony that looks down into the Onze-Lieve-Vrouwekerk (▷ 78), one of the oldest parts of the building.

Brangwyn Museum (Arents Huis) The Arents House, opposite the coach house, is home to the Brangwyn Museum. Here you'll find the world's largest collection of work by Frank Brangwyn (1867–1956).

One of the cathedral's Brussels tapestries (below); looking to the high altar (right)

Kathedraal St.-Salvator

The Kathedraal St.-Salvator, together with the belfry and the Onze-Lieve-Vrouwekerk, towers above Bruges. The splendid sculptures and tapestries inside are a reminder of the cathedral's long and eventful history.

The cathedral A house of prayer existed here as early as the 9th century; it was dedicated to St. Saviour and to St. Eloi, who is believed to have founded an earlier wooden church here in 660. The present cathedral was built near the end of the 13th century. It was damaged by several fires, and in 1798 many of its treasures were stolen by the French, who put the building and its contents up for auction the following year. However, wealthy Brugeans bought a lot back. The neo-Romanesque top was added to the remarkable tower in 1844–46 and the spire in 1871. The oldest sections of the tower date back to 1127.

Sculptures and tapestries The large statue of *God the Father* (1682) by Artus Quellinus is one of the best baroque sculptures in Bruges. The doors of the Shoemakers' chapel, as well as the sculptures in the Cross chapel and the Peter and Paul chapel, are superb examples of late Gothic oak carving. Six of the eight 18th-century tapestries were woven in Brussels.

The museum There are great pieces of 15th-century Flemish art among the 120 paintings in the museum, as well as gold and manuscripts.

THE BASICS

✚ b3
✉ Zuidzandstraat
☎ 050 33 61 88
🕐 Mon–Sat 10–1, 2–5.30, Sun 11.30–12, 2–5. Museum Sun–Fri 2–5
🚌 All city buses
♿ Very good
💶 Cathedral free; museum moderate

HIGHLIGHTS

● *Martyr's Death of St. Hippolytus*, Dirk Bouts' triptych (1470–75)
● *Last Supper*, Pieter Pourbus
● 14th-century *Tanner's Panel*
● *The Mother of Sorrows*
● Baroque statue of *God the Father*
● Eekhout Cross in Shoemakers' chapel
● Eight tapestries by Jasper van der Borght

Markt

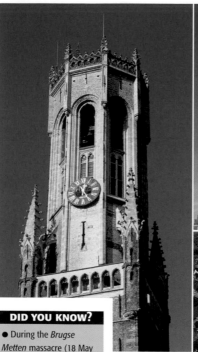

The Belfort (Belfry), emblematic of Bruges' medieval power and freedom, dominates the city's main square, the Markt (Market). The square is ringed with Gothic and neo-Gothic buildings.

The city's core This square, with its attractive historic buildings, has always been at the heart of Bruges. There's been a weekly market here since 1200; today it's flowers and food on Wednesday mornings. The old Central Post Office and neo-Gothic Provinciaal Hof (Provincial Government Palace) stand on the site of the former Waterhallen, a huge covered dock. Across Sint-Amandstraat is Craenenburg House, where Maximilian of Austria was locked up in 1488. The square's north side was once lined with tilers' and fishmongers' guildhalls.

Stunning buildings with colorful cafés and striking monuments surround the Markt

Heroes There is a bronze statue (1887) of two medieval Bruges heroes, Jan Breydel and Pieter de Coninck, who in 1302 led the *Brugse Metten*, the massacre of hundreds of occupying French soldiers by Flemish workers. The same year saw the rebellion of the Flemish against the French king, Philip IV, culminate at the Battle of the Golden Spurs, resulting in Flanders' independence.

The Hallen and Belfry The origins of the Hallen (town hall and treasury) and the Belfry (called the Belfort or Halletoren in Bruges) go back to the 13th century, when the Hallen were originally the seat of the municipality and the city's treasury. From the balcony, the bailiff read the "Hallen commands," while the bells warned citizens of approaching danger or enemies.

THE BASICS

✚ b3
✉ Markt
☎ 050 44 87 43
🕐 Belfry daily 9.30–6
🍴 Restaurants and tea rooms nearby
🚌 All city buses
✋ Belfry expensive
❓ Carillon concerts all year Wed, Sat, Sun 11am, mid-Jun to mid-Sep, Mon and Wed 9pm

Onze-Lieve-Vrouwekerk

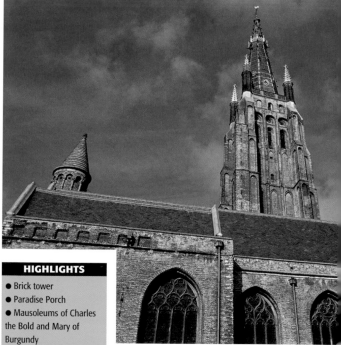

HIGHLIGHTS

● Brick tower
● Paradise Porch
● Mausoleums of Charles the Bold and Mary of Burgundy
● *Madonna and Child*, Michelangelo
● *The Adoration of the Shepherds*, Pieter Pourbus
● *Our Lady of the Seven Sorrows*, probably by Adriaen Isenbrandt
● *The Transfiguration of Mount Tabor*, Gerard David

TIP

● Attend a church service in the Onze-Lieve-Vrouwekerk. The acoustics are excellent, and your eyes can linger on the great Gothic architecture.

Beneath the monumental brick tower in the Church of our Lady, the religious feeling is palpable, heightened by the aroma of incense, the sculptures and the stunning paintings all around you.

One of Bruges' seven wonders Although there was a chapel here about 1,000 years ago, the choir and facade on Mariastraat date from the 13th century, and the aisles and superbly restored Paradise Porch from the 14th and 15th centuries. The church's most striking feature is the tower, 400ft (122m) high, begun in the 13th century.

Artworks The star attraction is the *Madonna and Child* by Michelangelo (1475–1564). Other sculptures include a rococo pulpit

From left: The Church of our Lady dates from the 13th century; inside you can see Michelangelo's Madonna and Child

(1743) by the Bruges painter Jan Garemijn, some fine altars and the Lanchals monument in the Lanchals chapel (15th century) The prayer balcony connected to the Gruuthuse mansion (▷ 74) enabled the lords of Gruuthuse to attend services directly from home. The church contains some important 16th-century Flemish paintings, including works by Gerard David, Pieter Pourbus and Adriaen Isenbrandt. The valuable *Katte of Beversluys*, a monstrance weighing 7lb (3kg), is kept in the sacristy.

Mausoleums Both Charles the Bold, who died in 1477, and Mary of Burgundy, who died in 1482 after a hunting fall, are buried here in superb adjacent mausoleums. Excavations revealed beautiful 16th-century frescoes in other tombs.

THE BASICS

- ✚ b3
- ✉ Mariastraat
- 🕐 Mon–Sat 9.30–5, Sun 1.30–5; no sightseeing during church services
- 🚌 1, 2, 4, 6, 11–16
- ♿ Very good
- ✋ Church free, museum moderate
- ❓ Weekend services: Sat 5.30, Sun 11am

St.-Janshospitaal en Memling Museum

The Hans Memling works on show here are 15th-century landmarks in the history of art and are not to be missed. The building that houses them is also a gem.

The hospital St. John's, founded in the 12th century, is one of Europe's oldest preserved hospices where nuns cared for the bodies and souls of the poor. The Gothic Maria Portal (*c.*1270) on Mariastraat is the original gate. Subsequent buildings include a tower, central ward, brewery, monastery, bathhouse, cemetery (all 14th century), St. Cornelius Chapel (15th century) and a convent for the hospital's sisters (1539). The 17th-century dispensary, with exhibits of remedies, and the church are worth visiting. The wards have been renovated and some were converted into cafés and shops.

The Memling Museum was once a medieval hospital

The Memling masterpieces As St. John's reputation as a hospital grew, so did its wealth. Its funds were invested, with inspiration, in the works of Hans Memling, a German painter who had settled in Bruges by 1465 and died one of its richest citizens in 1494. Four of the six works on display here were commissioned by St. John's friars and sisters, the most famous being the *Ursula Shrine* (1489), a reliquary in the shape of a church, gilded and painted with scenes from the life of St. Ursula and the *St. John Altarpiece* (1479). The main panel of this triptych depicts the Virgin and Child enthroned, with the side wings showing St. John the Baptist and St. John the Evangelist. It was commissioned for the main altar of the chapel. Other commissions include the *Adoration of the Magi* (1475) and *The Lamentation of Christ* (1480).

THE BASICS

+ b3
- Mariastraat 38
- 050 44 87 43
- Tue–Sun 9.30–5
- 1, 2, 4, 6, 11–16
- Restaurants nearby
- Very good
- Expensive

De Vesten en Poorten

TOP 25

Kruispoort gate (left) and Gentpoort gate (right)

THE BASICS

➕ Gentpoort c–d4;
Kruispoort d3;
Smedenpoort a3;
Ezelpoort b2

TIPS

● The ramparts of Bruges (6.5km/4 miles long) were laid out as parks in the 19th century and are ideal for a good jogging session or pleasant walk.
● Alternatively, rent a bicycle (▷ 118) as there are cycling routes all along.

DID YOU KNOW?

● The statue of St. Adrian (1448, remodeled in 1956) on Gentpoort was carved by Jan van Cutsegem to ward off plague.
● Smedenpoort's bronze skull (hung there in 1911) replaces the real skull of a traitor.
● There were 25 windmills in Bruges in 1562.

To understand Bruges' layout, take a bicycle ride or walk around its walls, especially on the east side, where the gates, ramparts, windmills and canals give the impression of containing the city, as they have done for 600 years.

Fortified Bruges Bruges' original fortifications (de Vesten en Poorten) date back to AD1000, but nothing survives of the six original bastion gates beyond an inscription on Blinde Ezelstraat. Between 1297 and 1300, as the medieval city grew increasingly wealthy, new defenses were built; of the seven new gates, four survive, two in the east—Kruispoort (Cross Gate, 1402), with a drawbridge, and Gentpoort (Ghent Gate, 14th century) with twin towers—and two in the west—Bruges' only two-way gate, Smedenpoort (Blacksmiths' Gate, 14th century) and Ezelpoort (Donkeys' Gate, rebuilt in the 17th and 18th centuries).

Blowing in the wind The eastern ramparts were used as platforms for windmills, but only four mills remain between Kruispoort and Dampoort. The first mill when viewed coming from Kruispoort, Bonne Chiere (Good Show), was built in 1888 and reconstructed in 1911, but has never worked. The second, St.-Janshuismolen (St. John's House Mill; ▷ 86) was built by bakers in 1770. The third, De Nieuwe Papegaai (New Parrot), a 1790 oil mill, was moved to Bruges from Beveren in 1970. A fourth, rebuilt in the 1990s, is near Dampoort.

More to See

BASILIEK VAN HET HEILIG-BLOED

holyblood.com

This is a double church, with the 12th-century Romanesque St. Basilius Chapel downstairs, shrouded in mystery and rich with the atmosphere of the Middle Ages. The Reliquary of the Holy Blood is kept in the upstairs 19th-century neo-Gothic chapel. The crystal phial containing two drops of holy blood is contained in a gold and silver reliquary, richly decorated with pearls and precious stones. One of the holiest relics of medieval Europe, it is believed to have been brought here by Thierry d'Alsace, who was given it by the Patriarch of Jerusalem during the Second Crusade. It is believed that at first the blood in the phial liquefied every Friday, a miracle that stopped in the 15th century. The relic is displayed on Friday, before and after the Mass, for veneration by the faithful. The reliquary is carried around the city every year during the Procession of the Holy Blood. The museum contains paintings, tapestries and other silver reliquaries.

🔢 c3 ✉ Burg 10 🕐 Daily 9.30–12.30, 2–5.30. Closed during services 🚌 All buses to the Markt 🦽 None 🎫 Church free, museum inexpensive ❓ Sun services 11am. Adoration of the Holy Blood Wed 10–11am

BROUWERIJ DE HALVE MAAN

halvemaan.be

De Halve Maan is the only family brewery still working in the heart of Bruges and it's been running since 1856. A tour takes about 45 minutes, after which you can try the delicious local Brugse Zot (Mad Bruges) beer and there's a restaurant open for lunch.

🔢 b4 ✉ Walplein 26 ☎ 050 44 42 22 🕐 Tours daily between 11am and 4pm (Sat 5) 🚌 1, 2 💰 Expensive

CONCERTGEBOUW

concertgebouw.be

Finished in 2002 to celebrate Bruges as the European City of

Learn how beer is made at Brouwerij de Halve Maan

Concertgebouw

Culture, this impressive structure has become the city's fourth landmark. It has a concert hall seating 1300 and a small hall for chamber music.

🔲 b3 ✉ 't Zand 34 ☎ 050 47 69 99 🕐 During performances 🚌 All city buses

DIAMANTMUSEUM

diamondmuseum.be

This private museum tells the history of Bruges as the oldest diamond hub in Europe. The art of diamond polishing was invented in the 15th century by the local gold-smith Lodewijk van Berquem. Diamonds are one of Belgium's main export products and the museum features the imaginary workshop of Berquem, a replica of the crown of Margaret of York made in Bruges, mining equipment, diamond manufacturing tools used in Belgium, and thousands of real diamonds.

🔲 b–c4 ✉ Katelijnestraat 43 ☎ 050 34 20 56 🕐 Daily 10.30–5.30. Closed middle 2 weeks Jan 🚌 1

HISTORIUM

historium.be

Get immersed in medieval Bruges as you wander through seven cleverly themed rooms that tell of the city's Golden Age. Film, music and special effects enhance the experience.

🔲 c3 ✉ Markt 1 ☎ 050 27 03 11 🕐 Daily 10–6 🚌 Any bus to the Markt ♿ Good, but phone for information 🖐 Expensive

JAN VAN EYCKPLEIN

Standing at the heart of this picturesque square is a statue of the famous Flemish painter Jan van Eyck (1370–1441). At No. 2 is the old Tolhuis (Toll House), where the ships coming into Bruges' inner port had to pay taxes on their cargo. The square overlooks the beautiful Spiegelrei, with some of the city's grandest houses on the canal. In the nearby square of the Woensdagmarkt is a statue of the painter, Hans Memling.

🔲 c2 ✉ Jan van Eyckplein 🚌 4 🖐 Free

The Museum voor Volkskunde

JERUZALEMKERK
The plan for this 15th-century church was inspired by the Basilica of the Holy Sepulcher in Jerusalem. The remarkable interior includes fine stained-glass windows and the tomb of the Genoese merchant Anselmus Adornes and his wife, who built the almshouses next to the church. These now house an exhibition about the Adornes family.
➕ c–d2 ✉ Peperstraat 3a 🕐 Mon–Sat 10–5 🚌 6, 16 ♿ Good 🎫 Moderate

MINNEWATER
South of the Begijnhof (▷ 66) is the Minnewater—the Lovers' Lake. This was the outer port before the river silted up and cut Bruges off from the sea. It is named after a woman called Minna who, according to legend, fell in love with a man her father did not like. Minna hid in the woods around the lake, and died there before her lover could rescue her. Her lover parted the waters and buried her under the lake. Next to the lake is a delightful park, with a sculpture garden and free concerts in summer.
➕ b4 ✉ Arsenaalstraat 🕐 Open 24 hours 🍴 Café-restaurant 🚌 All buses to train station ♿ Good 🎫 Free

MUSEUM ONZE-LIEVE-VROUW-TER POTTERIE
This wonderful little museum is in a former hospital dating from the 13th to 17th centuries. There are sculptures, 15th- and 16th-century paintings, tapestries and furniture. The church has one of Bruges' finest baroque interiors.
➕ c1 ✉ Potterierei 79 ☎ 050 44 87 43 🕐 Tue–Sun 9.30–12.30, 1.30–5 🚌 4, 14, 43 ♿ Very good 🎫 Moderate

MUSEUM VOOR VOLKSKUNDE
Bruges' past is recalled in these beautifully restored 17th-century almshouses, originally built for shoemakers. Period rooms, including an old pharmacy, a shoemaker's workshop and a small sugar bakery. You can also see the costumes people wore and learn about the

The beautiful St.-Jakobskerk founded in the 13th century

popular worship. After the visit, have a rest in the traditional inn "De Zwarte Kat."

🔆 c2 ✉ Balstraat 43 ☎ 050 44 87 43 🕐 Tue–Sun 9.30–5 🍴 Medieval inn De Zwarte Kat 🚌 6, 16 🚹 Good 💷 Moderate

ST.-JAKOBSKERK

This beautiful church was founded c.1240 in a district of rich Brugean families and foreign delegations, who all made generous donations for the decoration of the building. The church has a rich collection of paintings by Pieter Pourbus, Lancelot Blondeel and several anonymous Flemish Primitives.

🔆 b2 ✉ Sint-Jakobsplein 1 ☎ 050 33 68 41 🕐 Apr–Sep daily 10–1, 2–6 🚌 3, 13

ST.-JANSHUISMOLEN

The only one of Bruges' four windmills that can be visited, St.-Janshuismolen was built by a group of bakers in 1770 and acquired by the city of Bruges in 1914. It still grinds grain in summer. Inside is a museum.

🔆 d2 ✉ Kruisvest ☎ 050 44 87 11 🕐 May–Sep Tue–Sun 9.30–12, 1.30–5 🚌 6, 16 🚹 None 💷 Inexpensive

SINT-WALBURGAKERK

Pieter Huyssens built this splendid Jesuit baroque church between 1619 and 1642, and the 17th-century oak pulpit is astonishing. In summer the church is open to the public at night, with special lighting and music. Another fine feature of this building are the white communion rails.

🔆 c2 ✉ Sint-Maartensplein 🕐 Daily 1–6 🚌 6, 16 🚹 None 💷 Free

VISMARKT

The fish market was built in 1821 and North Sea and Atlantic Ocean fish and seafood is still sold here from Tuesday to Saturday. The market has a few good fish restaurants, and shops where you can pick up a *stokvis* (a snack of dried fish) or *maatje* (cured herring with onions).

🔆 c3 🕐 Tue–Sat 8–1.30 🚌 All buses to the Markt 💷 Free

A view over the canal from the Vismarkt

Lesser-known Bruges

Discover the canals and quiet medieval streets of this less-touristy corner of Bruges, with its low houses and beautiful churches.

DISTANCE: 2km (1.2 miles) **ALLOW:** 2 hours

START

SINT-WALBURGAKERK
✚ c2 🚌 6, 16

END

BURG
✚ c3 🚌 All buses to Markt

❶ Start at Boomgaardstraat, with the baroque church of St. Walburga (▷ 86). Turn right onto Hoornstraat, then right on Verwersdijk.

❽ At the end of the street is Vismarkt (▷ 86), with its fish market. To the right, an alley under the arch leads to the Burg (▷ 68).

❷ Cross the bridge and walk along St.-Annakerkstraat to Jeruzalemstraat, with the Jeruzalemkerk (▷ 84), with its unique, and often macabre, artifacts beckoning to the right.

❼ Before the end of Langestraat turn left onto Predikherenstraat, just past the bridge, and turn right to Groenerei, one of Bruges' loveliest corners.

❸ Walk along Balstraat, with the Museum voor Volkskunde (▷ 85). Cross Rolweg to Carmersstraat and turn right.

❻ On the corner with Rolweg is a museum dedicated to the Flemish poet Guido Gezelle (1830–99) and farther along, the Bonne Chiere windmill. At the Kruispoort, turn right onto Langestraat.

❹ No. 85 is the English convent; No. 174 is the old Schuttersgilde St.-Sebastiaan, the archers' guildhouse; and straight ahead on Kruisvest is the St.-Janshuis windmill (▷ 86).

❺ Take a right along Kruisvest.

Shopping

'T APOSTELIENTJE

apostelientje.be

This small store offers professional advice about lacemaking. You can buy the tools you need to make lace, along with ready-made old and modern lace.

🔲 c2 ✉ Balstraat 11 ☎ 050 33 78 60 🕐 Tue 1–5, Wed–Sat 9.30–12.15, 1.15–5, Sun 9.30–1 🚌 6, 16

THE BOTTLE SHOP

thebottleshop.be

Step through the door of this store and you enter a cornucopia of beer, bottles and glasses. Many of the hundreds of beers are Belgian, including lambic and gueuze beers.

🔲 c3 ✉ Wollestraat 13 ☎ 050 34 99 80 🕐 Daily 10–6.30 🚌 All buses to Markt

BRUGS DIAMANTHUIS

diamondhouse.net

The technique of diamond polishing is attributed to the mid-15th-century Bruges goldsmith van Berquem, and Bruges was Europe's first diamond city. This shop offers a large selection of quality diamonds and diamond jewelry. See also the Diamantmuseum (▷ 84).

🔲 c4 ✉ Cordoeaniersstraat 5 ☎ 050 34 41 60 🕐 Daily 10.30–5.30 🚌 6, 16

THE CHOCOLATE LINE

thechocolateline.be

Follow the story of chocolate, from tree to bar, and discover some unusual and exciting flavors at this imaginative shop.

🔲 b3 ✉ Simon Stevinplein 19 ☎ 050 34 10 90 🕐 Tue–Sat 9.30-6.30, Sun-Mon 10.30-6.30 🚌 2, 3, 4, 13

CHOCOLATIER DEPLA POL

poldepla.be

This store sells some of the city's finest hand-made chocolates, particularly truffles, florentines and marzipan. The window displays fantastic sculptues.

🔲 b3 ✉ Mariastraat 20 ☎ 050 34 74 12 🕐 Daily 10–6 🚌 1

D'S DELDYCKE TRAITEURS

deldycke.be

A quality deli with Belgian specials as well as the best foods from around the world. Buy to take away, stock up for a picnic or eat at the shared table.

🔲 c3 ✉ Wollestraat 23 ☎ 050 33 43 35 🕐 Wed–Mon 10–6.30 🚌 All buses to Markt

DIKSMUIDS BOTERHUIS

diksmuidsboterhuis.be

The oldest cheese store in Bruges with hams and sausages hanging from the ceiling, and a superb selection of Belgian and French cheeses and breads.

🔲 b3 ✉ Geldmuntstraat 23 ☎ 050 33 32 43 🕐 Tue–Sat 10–12.30, 2–6.30 🚌 All buses to Markt

DILLE & KAMILLE

dille-kamille.be

A wonderful store with simple white and rustic household ware, herbs and spices,

---

FABRICS AND LACE

In the 13th century, Belgium was already famous for woven fabrics and intricate tapestries, made from English wool and exported as far as Asia. By the 16th century, Brussels was renowned for the fine quality of its lace. Lace remains one of the most popular traditional souvenirs of Brussels and Bruges but few Belgians learn the craft today. As a result, there is not enough handmade lace to meet the demand, and what there is has become very expensive. Many shops now sell lace made in China, which costs less but is inferior.

wooden toys, cake moulds and cooking accessories—great for gifts or as a treat for yourself.

🏠 b3 ✉ Simon Stevinplein 17–18 ☎ 050 34 11 80 🕐 Mon–Sat 9.30–6.30, Sun 11–6.30 🚌 All city buses

L'HEROÏNE

lheroine.be

The best selection of Belgian fashion is found at this small but excellent store, stocking Dries Van Noten, Kaat Tilley, and Frieda Degeyter.

🏠 b3 ✉ Noordzandstraat 32 ☎ 050 33 56 57 🕐 Mon–Wed 10–1, 2–6, Thu–Sat 10–6 🚌 All city buses

KANTCENTRUM (LACE CENTRE)

kantcentrum.eu

See historical exhibits or watch an afternoon lacemaking demonstration. Lacemaking materials are also sold.

🏠 d2 ✉ Balstraat 16 ☎ 050 33 00 72 🕐 Mon–Sat 9.30–5. Lacemaking demonstrations Mon–Sat 2–5 💶 Moderate 🚌 6, 16

MALESHERBES

A small shop specializing in French wines, foie gras from Périgord in France, home-made terrines and farmhouse cheeses. Next door is a small bistro.

🏠 b4 ✉ Stoofstraat 5 ☎ 050 33 69 24 🕐 Wed–Sun 12–3, 7–10 🚌 1

THE OLD CURIOSITY SHOP

This tiny shop has a very large collection of old postcards, posters, secondhand books and old photographs.

🏠 b4 ✉ Walstraat 8 ☎ 050 34 35 91 🕐 Wed–Mon 10–6 🚌 1, 11

DE REYGHERE

dereyghere.be

If you're short on reading material head here for books in Flemish, French,

English and German, and international newspapers and magazines.

🏠 b3 ✉ Markt 12 ☎ 050 33 34 03 🕐 Mon–Sat 9–6 🚌 All buses to Markt

ROMBAUX

rombaux.be

A lovely old-fashioned store with sheet music, CDs and instruments.

🏠 c3 ✉ Mallebergplaats 13 ☎ 050 33 25 75 🕐 Mon 2–6.30, Tue–Fri 10–12.30, 2–6.30, Sat 10–6 🚌 All buses to Markt

SPEGELAERE

Bruges' best-kept secret: all chocolates are made on site; don't miss the famous "Bruges Cobblestones."

🏠 b2 ✉ Ezelstraat 94 ☎ 050 33 60 52 🕐 Tue–Sat 8.30–12, 1.30–6.30, Sun 9–1 🚌 3, 13

DE STRIEP

striepclub.be

De Striep specializes in comic strips, mainly Belgian and French, but some English and some set in Bruges.

🏠 c4 ✉ Katelijnestraat 42 ☎ 050 33 71 12 🕐 Tue–Sat 10–12.30, 1.30–7 🚌 1

YANNICK DE HONDT

yannickdehondt.be

Stylish antiques shop with a mix of authentic European antiques and African tribal art and artefacts.

🏠 b3 ✉ St.-Salvatorskerkhof 9 ☎ 0475 65 30 58 🕐 Mon–Sat 2–6 🚌 2, 3, 4, 13, 14

BELGIAN COOKIES

Pain à la Grècque is a light crispy cookie covered in tiny bits of sugar, while *speculoos* is a finer version of gingerbread. The *couque de Dinant* is a hard, bread-like cookie that comes in beautiful shapes—windmills, rabbits, cars and more.

Entertainment and Nightlife

CACTUS CLUB
cactusmusic.be
The main venue in town for rock, jazz and world music, with the Cactus Club@ MaZ hosting 900 people. The Cactus Club also organizes an open-air festival in Minnewaterpark during the second weekend of July, as well as other summer festivals in several central locations.
🔖 a3 ✉ MaZ, Magdalenastraat 27, Sint-Andries ☎ 050 33 20 14 🚌 2, 7, 88, 94

CONCERTGEBOUW
A top-quality music venue (▷ 83).

CULTUURCENTRUM
ccbrugge.be
Seven venues under one name are here, including the renovated Stadsschouwburg (▷ this page) and MaZ, a platform for youth culture. The performances in all these venues include contemporary dance, world music, drama, comedy and classical music concerts, as well as exhibitions.
🔖 b3 ✉ St.-Jacobsstraat 20–26 ☎ 050 44 30 40. Box office: 050 44 30 60 🕐 Box office: Tue–Fri 1–5 🚌 All city buses

JAZZ & BLUES BAR 27 B FLAT
27bflat.be
There's live music, tasty food, a good atmosphere and even a garden here, all tucked away in the heart of Bruges.
🔖 b3 ✉ Katelijnstraat 27b ☎ 479 29 74 29 🕐 Wed–Fri 6pm–1am, Sat 3pm–1am, Sun 3pm–midnight 🚌 11, 12

KINEPOLIS BRUGGE
kinepolis.be
Kinepolis has eight cinemas showing recent and classic films in their original language.
🔖 Off map at a4 ✉ Koning Albert 1-laan 200, Sint-Michiels ☎ 050 30 50 00 🚌 27

LUMIÈRE
lumiere.be
This cinema shows mainly foreign art-house films and better Belgian productions, without popcorn or advertising. Part of the complex is De Republiek (▷ 92), a café that is hugely popular with locals.
🔖 b2–3 ✉ St.-Jacobsstraat 36 ☎ 050 34 34 65 🚌 All city buses

STADSSCHOUWBURG
ccbrugge.be
Beautifully restored 19th-century municipal theater staging dance, drama, concerts and international productions.
🔖 b2–3 ✉ Vlamingstraat 29 ☎ 050 44 30 60 🚌 All city buses

LE TRAPPISTE
letrappistebrugge.com
Friendly and beer-savvy staff add to the welcoming atmosphere of this vaulted cellar bar with some of the strongest brews you're likely to taste—head there after a filling meal for a nightcap.
🔖 b2 ✉ Kuipersstraat 33 🕐 Daily 5pm–1am 🚌 2, 3, 4, 5

DE WERF
kaap.be
Well-established avant-garde arts venue that often stages live concerts of experimental jazz.
🔖 b1–2 ✉ Werfstraat 108 ☎ 050 33 05 29 🚌 41, 42

LBGTQ
Bruges is a friendly city and its bars and restaurants are very mixed. For a relaxed beer (there are 80+ types to choose from) try @The Pub (✉ Hallestraat 4 ☎ 484 919 654), which holds an LGBT Talking Café on the first Friday of the month.

Where to Eat

BISTRO BRUUT (€€€)

bistrobruut.be

With a modern twist on traditional
Flemish dishes, this award-winning
gastro-bistro by the romantic Meebrug
has a fixed tasting menu, the dishes
selected and introduced by the passion-
ate chef/owner Bruno Timperman.

➕ c3 ✉ Meestraat 9 ☎ 050 69 55 09
🕐 Mon–Fri 12–1.30, 7–8.45 🚌 6, 16

BREYDEL DE CONINC (€€)

restaurant-breydel.be

Locals claim this restaurant serves the
best *moules-frites* in town as well as
other fish dishes, including bouillabaisse,
eel Provençale and lobster with
garlic butter.

➕ c3 ✉ Breidelstraat 24 ☎ 050 33 97 46
🕐 Thu–Tue 12–2.30, 6.30–10 🚌 All buses to
Markt

'T BRUGS BEERTJE (€)

brugsbeertje.be

The place for true beer lovers, with 300
traditionally brewed Belgian beers—
many of them rare and for sale only
here, and all served in their special
glass. Staff are knowledgeable and
happy to advise you on your selection.
The atmosphere is as Belgian as can be.
Full meals are not served, but you can
order snacks and cheese to enhance
the beer tasting.

➕ b3 ✉ Kemelstraat 5 ☎ 050 33 96 16
🕐 Mon–Tue, Thu, Sun 4pm–midnight, Fri–Sat
4pm–1am 🚌 All buses

CAFEDRAAL (€€–€€€)

cafedraal.be

This hidden seafood restaurant serves
waterzooi and an excellent North Sea
bouillabaisse, in a splendid setting.
There is a torchlit garden terrace.

➕ b3 ✉ Zilverstraat 38 ☎ 050 34 08 45
🕐 Tue–Sat lunch, dinner 🚌 All city buses

CAFÉ VLISSINGHE (€)

cafevlissinghe.be

Reputedly the oldest café in Bruges,
built around 1515, this is popular with
locals as well as visitors. The atmosphere is relaxed and easygoing.

➕ c2 ✉ Blekerstraat 2 ☎ 050 34 37 37
🕐 Wed–Sat 11–10 🚌 4, 14

CHRISTOPHE (€€)

christophe-brugge.be

Belgians eat pretty early, but if you're
looking for a place to eat after a film or
concert then come here. This great bistro serves Belgian and French dishes
with flair. It's popular so call ahead.

➕ c3 ✉ Garenmarkt 34 ☎ 050 34 48 92
🕐 Mon, Thu 6–11, Fri–Sun 6pm–1am
🚌 1, 11

DEN DYVER (€€)

dyver.be

Dishes here are inventive and prepared
with Belgian beer. The style is old
Flemish, and the view from the terrace
is memorable.

➕ b3 ✉ Dijver 5 ☎ 050 33 60 69
🕐 Tue–Sat 12–2.30, 6–10 🚌 1, 6, 11, 16

BEER IN BRUGES

In the heart of town. Brouwerij De Halve
Maan (✉ Walplein 26 ☎ 050 44 42 22,
▷ 83) brews Straffe Hendrik, a wheat beer
with a sweet aroma that's good with a slice
of lemon.

L'ESTAMINET (€)

estaminet-brugge.be

Atmospheric old-style pub with a good snack menu. The spaghetti Bolognese is legendary. In the summer there's a popular terrace by Astrid Park.

➕ c3 ✉ Park 5 ☎ 050 33 09 16 🕐 Tue, Wed, Fri–Sun 11.30am until late, Thu from 4pm 🚌 All buses to Markt

DE FLORENTIJNEN (€€€)

deflorentijnen.be

In a much-restored house built in 1430, that originally housed the wealthy Florentine merchant community in Bruges, this restaurant continues in a classy vein but with a light modern touch to both the decor and cuisine.

➕ b2 ✉ Academiestraat 1 ☎ 050 67 75 33 🕐 Tue–Sat lunch, dinner 🚌 4, 14, 43

DEN GOUDEN HARYNCK (€€€)

goudenharynck.be

The fine chef here prepares the freshest ingredients without too many frills. Offering imaginative French cuisine and fine wines in a stylish setting, the fixed-price menus are seasonal.

➕ b–c3 ✉ Groeninge 25 ☎ 050 33 76 37 🕐 Tue–Fri lunch, dinner, Sat dinner 🚌 1

JAN VAN EYCK (€€)

Start the day with a hearty breakfast, enjoy mussels for lunch, sample home-made pancakes in the afternoon and relish pan-fried salmon or a range of delicious steaks for dinner.

➕ c2 ✉ Jan van Eyckplein 12 ☎ 050 67 74 17 🕐 Daily 11–10 🚌 4, 14, 43

DE PLAATS (€–€€)

deplaats.be

A vegetarian restaurant with vegan options, serves soups, salads, pasta and tasty meat-free burgers

➕ c3 ✉ Wapenmakersstraat 5 ☎ 050 66 03 66 🕐 Mon 12–2, Thu–Fri 12–2, 6–9, Sat 6–9 🚌 All buses to Markt

DE REPUBLIEK (€–€€)

republiekbrugge.be

A large and popular bar with high ceilings, a garden in summer and a good selection of beers and international dishes.

➕ b3 ✉ St.-Jakobsstraat 36 ☎ 050 73 47 64 🕐 Daily 11am–1am or later (Thu from 4) 🚌 All city buses

ROCK FORT (€€€)

rock-fort.be

This fashionable restaurant offers well-prepared Mediterranean dishes with a bit of Belgian and fusion.

➕ c3 ✉ Langestraat 15 ☎ 050 33 41 13 🕐 Mon–Fri 12–2.30, 6.30–10.30. Closed Wed lunch 🚌 All city buses

DE STOVE (€€–€€€)

restaurantdestove.be

This intimate little restaurant on a pedestrian street is appreciated for its delicious fish, coming fresh from Zeebrugge, and home-made desserts. All the ingredients are local and the owners are welcoming. The high-quality food makes it very popular so make sure you reserve ahead.

➕ b3 ✉ Kleine Sint-Amandsstraat 4 ☎ 050 33 78 35 🕐 Fri–Tue 11.45–2, 5.45–9 🚌 All buses to Markt

TANUKI (€€€)

tanuki.be

Classic Japanese dishes in an authentic setting with plenty of wood, a rock-tiled floor and a bamboo garden. The sushi and tempura are excellent.

➕ c4 ✉ Oude Gentweg 1 ☎ 050 34 75 12 🕐 Wed–Sun 12–2, 6.30–9.30 🚌 1, 11

Farther Afield

Belgium is not a large country and many of its attractions are just a short train ride from Brussels or Bruges. Marvel at more medieval cities, cycle around the endlessly flat countryside or learn about former battles.

Damme

HIGHLIGHTS

- View from the church tower
- Wooden statues of apostles
- A bicycle ride in the surrounding countryside
- A waffle or pancake in a tearoom
- Browsing the bookstores

TIPS

- QuasiMundo (☎ 050 33 07 75; quasimundo.com) runs cycle tours from Bruges to Damme.
- Damme has declared itself a book town; you'll find books in French, Flemish and English.

When the port of Bruges dried up in the 12th century, the Bruges-Damme canal was dug and Damme became the city's new port. Sea ships went up to Damme and unloaded the goods on smaller ships to go to Bruges via the canal. The town flourished for the next hundred years.

Missing church Damme's most famous monument, the Onze-Lieve-Vrouwekerk, was built on a grand scale in 1225, but in the 18th century the upkeep costs were considered too enormous, so the part between the church tower and the still-existing part of the church was destroyed, except for the supporting arches—hence the strange shape of the church today. The interior reveals many treasures, including 13th-century wooden sculptures of

From left: Modern sculpture in front of Domsce church; sunrise over the waters

the apostles and a cross found by fishermen from Damme in the sea, outed every year at the Holy Blood procession. The tower gives views over the star-shaped ramparts of the city.

Town hall The elegant Gothic Stadhuis of 1464 has two punishment stones on the corner and some fine moldings inside the Council Hall and the Hall of Justice. In front of it, on the main square, is the 19th-century statue of the Flemish poet Jacob van Maerlant.

Food Many visitors come to Damme for lunch or dinner after a stroll or a bike ride. The many restaurants offer local fare such as Damme tart with apples, Damme sausages, *paling in 't groen* (river eel in a green sorrel sauce) and a semi-hard Damme cheese.

THE BASICS

🕂 See map ▷ 94

🚍 43 from Bruges' Markt

🚢 The *Lamme Goedzak* paddle steamer runs from Bruges' Noorweegse Kaai to Damme (30-minute sailing) from Apr–Sep, at 12, 2, 4 and 6 (☎ 050 28 86 10)

🛈 Huyse de Grote Sterre, Jacob van Maerlantstraat 3 (visitdamme.be)

Heysel

HIGHLIGHTS

● The Atomium exhibitions
● Spectacular views over
Brussels and beyond

TIP

● Have lunch at the
panoramic restaurant in the
top sphere, with splendid
views over Brussels
(☎ 02 479 5850; daily
10–5, dinner service
Mon–Sat 7–9.30). Brunch
on a warm Sunday on
the terrace is also
recommended.

**To celebrate Belgium's 100th birthday
in 1930, the Centenary Stadium and
Palais du Centenaire were built here.
But Heysel's most famous landmark is
the glitzy Atomium, the main pavilion
from the World Exhibition of 1958.**

The Atomium The Atomium was designed in
steel for Expo '58 by André Waterkeyn. Its nine
interconnecting spheres represent the atoms
of an iron crystal enlarged 165 billion times.
The monument (335ft/102m high) remains
an extraordinary sight, symbolizing the opti-
mism of its time. It was built to last a year, but
it became a Brussels landmark and a symbol
for Belgium. The upper sphere offers 360°
views across the city of Brussels and as far away
as Antwerp, making it the perfect setting for the

The Atomium has become a symbol of Brussels

Panorama bar and restaurant. Several other balls are used for temporary exhibitions.

Permanent exhibition *Atomium. From Symbol to Icon* tells the history of the pavilion and the events of Expo '58. Special exhibitions on the themes of Science, Progress and the Future are staged at the Atomium and have covered such diverse subjects as progressive architecture, modern design and environmental projects. It extends across three floors: two levels of the base sphere and the viewpoint on level 7.

All around The Stade Roi Baudouin hosts sports events and rock concerts, while the Palais du Centenaire is the Brussels Exhibition Center for fairs and events.

THE BASICS

See map ▷ 95
Atomium
atomium.be
✉ Place de l'Atomium
☎ 02 475 4775
🕐 Daily 10–6
✋ Expensive
🚇 Heysel/Heizel
♿ Few

Jardin Botanique Meise

HIGHLIGHTS

● The fabulous 13 glasshouses of the Plant Palace
● Garden walks
● The Orangery restaurant

TIP

● Take a stroll among oak and conifer trees, magnolias, rhododendrons and wild roses in the north-west section of the garden.

The Jardin Botanique Meise (formerly known as the National Botanic Garden of Belgium) is one of the largest botanical gardens in the world. It has more than 18,000 types of plants, a herbarium of 4 million species and a library of 70,000 botanical works and journals, all housed within 227 acres (92ha) of the grounds of the old Castle Bouchout at Meise.

Plant Palace   The Botanical Garden dates from the early 19th century when Belgium was in the control of the Dutch. Until 1958, the garden was located in the middle of Brussels on a site that is now the Botanical Garden of Brussels. Today's garden has an extensive complex of greenhouses, including the huge Plant Palace where individual greenhouses contain

Clockwise from top left: inside the greenhouse of the Plant Palace; studying a giant fern; giant water lilies; the gardens lie in the grounds of Castle Bouchout

fascinating specimens from areas such as the Mediterranean and the tropical rainforest. In the Evolution House you can trace the development of plants over the past 500 million years.

Conservation The range of species is outstanding and includes bamboos, fuchsias, orchids, hydrangeas and camellias. The Herbarium displays a summer spread of herbaceous perennials while there is even a garden full of plants used in traditional medicine. The Botanic Garden's extensive research programs have earned it an international reputation. The garden also has a restaurant—the Orangery— and a garden shop with an excellent array of plant books, postcards and floral calendars. You can also buy seeds, honey, preserves and even botanical jewelry.

THE BASICS

plantentuinmeise.be
* See map ▷ 95
* Nieuwelaan 38, 1860 Meise
* 02 260 0970
* Mid-Mar to mid-Oct daily 9.30–6.30; mid-Oct to mid-Mar 9.30–5
* De Lijn bus 250, 251 from Brussels
* Good
* Orangery restaurant (Mar–Oct daily 11–5.30)
* Moderate

More to See

BASILIQUE NATIONALE DU SACRÉ-COEUR

The art deco basilica's massive green dome is one of Brussels' landmarks. Built between 1905 and 1969, the world's fifth-largest church was meant to symbolize unity between Belgium's Flemish and French-speaking communities. The views from the dome are superb and worth the climb.

🔲 A1 ☒ Parvis de la Basilique 1 ☎ 02 421 1660 🕐 Daily 8–6 (until 5 in winter). Dome Mar–Oct Mon–Fri 9–5; Nov–Feb 10–4 🚇 Simonis, then bus 13 or 97 💵 Free; entry to the dome moderate

BOUDEWIJN SEAPARK

boudewijnseapark.be

A great amusement park for both younger kids and teenagers, with Europe's most sophisticated dolphinarium.

🔲 See map ▷ 94 ☒ A. De Baeckestraat 12, St.-Michiels ☎ 050 38 38 38 🕐 Apr– Jun Tue–Thu 10–5; Jul–Aug daily 10–6 but check online for further details 🚆 7, 17 from railway station 🔵 Good 💵 Expensive

BRUPARCK

minieurope.com

At the foot of the Atomium (▷ 98), Bruparck hosts Mini-Europe with working scale models of 350 of the European Union's famous sights.

🔲 See map ▷ 94 ☒ Boulevard du Centenaire 20, Heysel ☎ 02 478 0550 🕐 Daily 9.30–6 🚇 Heysel/Heizel 🔵 Good 💵 Expensive

LAEKEN

Laeken is home to the royal family, whose palace, the Château Royal, is closed to the public. The exquisite Serres Royales (Royal Greenhouses), with an amazing variety of tropical plants, are open during April and May.

🔲 See map ▷ 94 ☒ Boulevard de Smet de Naeyer 🚇 Stuyvenberg 🚆 Tram 7, 19

DE ZEVEN TORENTJES

This former 14th-century farm estate is now a children's farm.

🔲 See map ▷ 94 ☒ Canadaring 41, Assebroek ☎ 050 35 40 43 🕐 Daily sun- rise–sunset 🚆 2 💵 Free

Flowerbeds in front of the Basilique Nationale du Sacré-Coeur

Miniature London at Bruparck

Excursions

ANTWERP

Antwerp is a lively Flemish city, famous for Belgian fashion. Many top Belgian designers have their flagship stores in this city that even boasts a fashion museum (MoMu). For centuries Antwerp has been known as the diamond capital of the world and the exhibition at DIVA is scintillating.

Antwerp is also the city of Rubens, whose work can be seen at his house, the Rubenshuis, and at the wonderful Koninklijk Museum voor Schone Kunsten (Fine Arts Museum), which has a large collection of Flemish Primitives and works from Antwerp's Golden Age (17th century). M HKA (Museum of Contemporary Art) focuses on art from 1970 to the present. The heart of Antwerp is the Grote Markt square and the seven-aisled Onze-Lieve-Vrouwe Cathedral featuring some of Ruben's most powerful paintings. The main shopping street is the elegant Meir.

THE BASICS

visitantwerpen.be
Distance: 45km (27 miles) from Brussels; 105km (65 miles) from Bruges
Journey Time: 40 min (Brussels); 1 hour (Bruges)
🚆 Several trains an hour from Brussels and Bruges
ℹ️ Grote Markt 13 (tel 03 232 0103)

GHENT

Ghent is pretty much undiscovered compared to Bruges and Brussels, but it's a lively city full of Flemish architecture and art. With a large university, there is a young vibe and vibrant nightlife.

At the heart of the city is the Gravensteen, the impressive 12th-century medieval castle of the Counts of Flanders. A short walk away is the 16th-century Gothic Sint-Baafskathedraal, which displays the city's greatest treasure, Hubert and Jan van Eyck's *Adoration of the Mystic Lamb*. Across from the cathedral is the Lakenhalle, the 15th-century Cloth Hall, and the majestic Belfort (belfry tower), with great views over the city. Old Masters and Modernists hang side-by-side in MAK, the Museum voor Schone Kunsten (Fine Arts Museum).

THE BASICS

visitgent.be
Distance: 56km (35 miles) from Brussels; 42km (26 miles) from Bruges
Journey Time: 40 min (Brussels); 30 min (Bruges)
🚆 Several trains each hour from Bruges and Brussels
ℹ️ Sint-Veerleplein 5 (tel 09 266 5660)
🍴 Some of the city's best restaurants are in the narrow alleys of Patershol

IEPER AND WAR MEMORIALS

During the 12th century Ieper (Ypres) was an important cloth trade hub, together with Ghent and Bruges.

Many of Ieper's important monuments date from that time, including the Lakenhalle (Cloth Hall), with 48 doors giving access to the spacious halls, the adjacent Belfry (230ft/70m high) and the Gothic Sint-Maartens-kathedraal. During World War I, the city was bombarded for four years and reduced to ruins, while 500,000 soldiers died in the "Ypres Salient." The rebuilding of the city took more than 40 years and 170 war cemeteries in the area pay tribute to the fallen soldiers. The In Flanders Field Museum tells Ypres' story during World War I. The city's Heritage Walk and Ramparts Route, both well signed, are good trails to follow.

THE BASICS

toerismeieper.be
wo1.be
Distance: 100km
(62 miles) from Brussels;
50km (31 miles) from
Bruges
🚆 Several direct trains
each day from Brussels or
via Ghent (2 hours); from
Bruges change trains in
Kortrijk (1.5 hours)
ℹ️ Lakenhalle, Grote
Markt (tel 057 23 92 20)

OSTEND

This lively town is popular with Belgians, who come for a walk on the long beach on weekends, to eat in one of the many fish restaurants around the port or to spend the evening in one of the bars.

The royal family chose Ostend for their summer residence, which earned it the name "Queen of Belgian Beach Resorts." Now, the Royal Villa built by Léopold I has long been sold and has become a health clinic. Art lovers should pay a visit to the Mu.Zee, with its collection of Belgian art from 1830 to the present day and includes works by James Ensor and Flemish painters Permeke and Spilliaert. You can wander around Ensor's former house and studio, now called the James Ensor House. Explore the town's interesting history at the Stadsmuseum Oostende (Ostend City Museum) and in the museum ships *Mercator* and *Amandine,* berthed in the harbor.

THE BASICS

visitoostende.be
Distance: 100km
(62 miles) from Brussels;
30km (19 miles) from
Bruges
🚆 Direct train from
Brussels (1.5 hours); from
Bruges (20 min)
ℹ️ Monacoplein 2
(tel 059 70 11 99)

Ghent (left) is a vibrant city, full of Flemish architecture. Ostend (below) is one of Belgium's largest resorts

THE BASICS

walibi.be
Distance: 16km (10 miles) from Brussels
Journey Time: 25 min
✉ E411 Brussels-Namur, exit 6, in Wavres ☎ 010 42 15 00 🕐 Phone or check website for opening times 🚆 Train from Gare Schuman to Gare de Bierges on Ottignies/Louvain-la-Neuve line (short walk from station) 🚻 Few 💰 Very expensive

WALIBI

Walibi, formerly known as Six Flags Belgium, is a spectacular theme park near Brussels, with a wide range of rides and attractions for all ages.

Rides include the Pulsar, which rises to great heights, splashes through water and has three powerful propulsions reaching 62mph (100km/h) and Buzzsaw, a giant swing that has you hovering upside down. Another exhilarating ride is the Cobra, which propels riders at 75km/h (46mph) into a series of double spirals and loops. Tiki-Waka takes families on a swirling funcoaster that can reach 34 mph (55km/h), while team family have laser guns to fight off the monsters that appear in the Challenge of Tutankhamen. The Radja River ride has sharp bends and surprise waterfalls. Younger children have their own playgrounds.

THE BASICS

waterloo1815.be
Distance: 20km (12.5 miles) from Brussels
Journey Time: 20 min
🚆 Brussels-Charleroi line to Braine-l'Alleud station then bus W
🚌 365, W
ℹ Route de Lion, 1815, Braine-l'Alleud (tel 02 385 1912)
Visitor Center
☎ 02 385 1912

WATERLOO

Here is the famous battlefield where the Duke of Wellington defeated Napoleon Bonaparte on 18 June 1815, ending France's military domination of Europe.

Most people come to see the Butte du Lion (pictured above and below right), a grass-covered pyramid built by local women with soil from the battlefield to mark the spot where William of Orange, one of Wellington's commanders and later King of the Netherlands, was wounded. Climb the 226 steps for the views. At the foot of the mound is the Memorial 1815, a multi-sensory experience that tells the story from every angle. Next to it, the Panorama is a massive fresco depicting the battle with remarkable intensity. The Hougoumont Farm has a multimedia show. A motorway now cuts through the battlefield, but for a clearer idea of what happened, attend the re-enactment held every year in June.

Where to Stay

Whatever your tastes and budget, there's plenty of choice for places to stay in Brussels and Bruges. Options range from modern luxury to old-fashioned charm in canal-side buildings.

Introduction

Brussels and Bruges have a large choice of accommodations, from the most luxurious to the most simple. Standards are usually fairly high, but some hotels, in Brussels in particular, lack beauty or special character. Most places include breakfast in the overnight rate, but if it is not included, count on paying €5–€15 extra.

Brussels

As the European capital, Brussels has no shortage of hotels, but many of these are geared toward businesspeople. This means that there are a large number of the smarter chain hotels such as the Hilton, Marriott and Novotel. These hotels, and in fact most hotels in town, often offer lower rates on weekends and during the summer, when the bureaucrats leave town. All year round, but particularly in the spring and fall, it pays to reserve ahead, as the city fills up quickly. For the impulsive, the Brussels International tourist office, on the Grand Place, provides a free booking service.

Bruges

With its canal setting and air of romance, Bruges seems to be made for walking and most accommodations are within easy reach of the main sights. The city gets very full, especially during summer and for the Christmas market, so advance reservations are recommended. However, the Bruges Tourist Information offices at Markt, t'Zand and Stationsplein can help with their same-night booking service.

BED-AND-BREAKFAST

As an alternative to hotel accommodations, both Brussels and Bruges have an increasing number of charming bed-and-breakfasts. These are usually good quality and less expensive than hotels, and you get the chance to ask the owners for inside information on the best places to visit. Tourist offices can arrange B&B rooms or you can check the list of B&Bs on their website. In Brussels, Bed & Brussels (bnb-brussels.be) has an online booking service. They are a popular choice so book well ahead.

Budget Hotels

PRICES

Expect to pay under €100 per night for a double room in a budget hotel.

BRUSSELS

LES BLUETS
bluets.be

This small and friendly hotel is in a grand 19th-century building furnished with antiques. The eight rooms are individually decorated with objets d'art and breakfast is served at a communal table.

➕ E8 ✉ Rue Berckmans 124 ☎ 02 534 3983 🚇 Hôtel des Monnaies 🚌 48–55; tram 91–94

LA LÉGENDE
hotellalegende.com

An attractive and very good-value hotel, with the rooms all around an internal courtyard. It is ideally located near the Grand Place, as well as the bars and restaurants of St.-Géry.

➕ D–E5 ✉ Rue du Lombard 35 ☎ 02 512 8290 🚇 Bourse/Beurs 🚌 95, 48; tram 23, 55, 56, 81

MADE IN LOUISE
madeinlouise.com

This elegant boutique hotel in the art nouveau district has small but bright rooms set in a townhouse with a leafy courtyard.

➕ E8 ✉ Rue Veydt 40 ☎ 02 537 4033 🚇 Louise/Louiza

VINTAGE HOTEL
vintagehotel.be

A 1970s themed design hotel in a great location with brightly decorated rooms and a vintage Airstream on the patio.

➕ E7 ✉ Rue Dejonker 45 ☎ 02 533 9980 🚇 Hotel Des Monnaies or Louise/Louiza 🚌 Tram 92, 97

ZOOM HOTEL
zoomhotel.be

Arty décor with a photographic theme define this offbeat hotel, with its rooms done out in industrial chic and a bar serving good Belgian beers.

➕ E8 ✉ Rue de la Concorde 59 ☎ 02 515 0060 🚇 Louise/Louiza 🚌 54; tram 8, 93

BRUGES

B&B MARIE-PAULE GESQUIÈRE

An intimate B&B with three comfortable rooms in an ivy-clad house overlooking a park by the city walls and windmills. Breakfast is very good with eggs and Belgian chocolate.

➕ d2 ✉ Oostproosse 14 ☎ 050 33 92 46 🚌 4, 16

ECO-HOTEL FEVERY
hotelfevery.be

A charming family-run, environmentally conscious boutique hotel in a quiet area of town. Breakfast is made from local, fairtrade and organic produce.

➕ c2 ✉ Collaert Mansionstraat 3 ☎ 050 33 12 69 🚌 4, 14, 43, 90

HOTEL ACADEMIE
hotelacademie.be

On a quiet, cobblestoned street near the Minnewater (▷ 85), this mid-sized hotel has individually furnished rooms in three buildings around a spacious courtyard garden.

➕ b4 ✉ Wijngaardstraat 7–9 ☎ 050 33 22 66 🚌 11, 12

HOTEL BLA BLA
hotelblabla.com

A small, friendly hotel near Kathedraal St.-Salvator (▷ 75), with simply furnished rooms set around a courtyard.

➕ b3 ✉ 24–28 Dweersstraat ☎ 050 33 90 14 🚌 All buses to 't Zand

WHERE TO STAY BUDGET HOTELS

Mid-Range Hotels

BRUSSELS

LE 9 HOTEL CENTRAL
le9hotel.com
This cool and comfy hotel boasts chic design interiors behind its classical Brussels facade. Exposed brickwork and attractive wooden artifacts in the rooms set the tone for the modernist style.
🔳 E5 ✉ Rue des Colonies 10 ☎ 02 504 9910 🚇 Gare Centrale 🚌 29, 63, 65, 66

LE 9 HOTEL SABLON
9-hotel-sablon-brussels.be
A stylishly modern hotel with designer touches, the rooms are light and minimalist. It has an indoor swimming pool, sauna and hot tub.
🔳 E6 ✉ Rue de la Paille 2–8, Sablon ☎ 02 880 0701 🚋 Tram 92, 93

ARLEQUIN
florishotelarlequin.be
A three-star hotel close to the Grand Place, with comfortable rooms. A buffet breakfast is served in the 7th Heaven dining room.
🔳 E5 ✉ Rue de la Fourche 17–19 ☎ 02 514 1615 🚇 Bourse/Beurs, Gare Centrale/ Centraal Station

L'ART DE SEJOUR
artdesejour.com
This is an outstanding bed-and-breakfast, close to the Grand Place, with the quality of the rooms being more akin to that of a five-star hotel. This is not a family-friendly hotel.
🔳 E5 ✉ Rue des Bogards 12 ☎ 02 513 9755 🚇 Gare Centrale/Centraal Station 🚌 33, 86

ATLAS HOTEL
atlas-hotel.be
A sleekly modernized hotel with smartly furnished rooms in a quiet location, but within walking distance of the buzzing heart of the city.
🔳 D5 ✉ Rue du Vieux Marché aux Grains 30 ☎ 02 502 6006 🚇 Bourse/Beurs 🚌 89, 127, 128

HOTEL-CAFÉ PACIFIC
hotelcafepacific.com
A stylish small hotel with a bright modernist vibe. The showers and basins are sectioned off with a curtain so not to everyone's taste.
🔳 D5 ✉ Rue Antoine Dansaert 57 ☎ 02 833 3040 🚇 Bourse/Beurs 🚌 86, 126, 127

METROPOLE
metropolehotel.com
This grand hotel, opened in 1895, has wonderful architecture in the public spaces. The bedrooms are more simple but very comfortable.
🔳 E4 ✉ Place de Brouckère 31 ☎ 02 217 2300 🚇 De Brouckère 🚋 Tram 3, 4, 31, 32

MONTY
monty-hotel.be
Convenient for the EU Quarter and Le Cinquantenaire, this small boutique hotel has spacious rooms, meticulously designed in a modernist warm style. The rooms are furnished with designs by Philippe Starck, A. Castiglioni and Ingo Maurer, among others.
🔳 Off map J6 ✉ Boulevard Brand Whitlock 101 ☎ 02 734 5636 🚇 Georges-Henri

NOGA
nogahotel.com
Tranquil, charming hotel located in the Ste.-Catherine district, near the fashionable hangouts on the rue

Dansaert. Breakfast is a continental buffet served in a nautical-themed room.
➕ D4 ✉ Rue du Béguinage 38 ☎ 02 218 6763 🚇 Ste.-Catherine/St.-Katelijne

WELCOME

hotelwelcome.com

Ideally situated in the popular Ste.-Catherine area, within walking distance of the Grand Place and the lively Place St.-Géry (▷ 38), here each of the exotic and theatrical rooms is decorated in the style of a far-off land.
➕ D4 ✉ Quai au Bois à Brûler 23 ☎ 02 219 9546 🚇 Ste.-Catherine/St.-Katelijne

▷ 38

BRUGES

ADORNES

adornes.be

A quiet three-star hotel in a beautiful old Flemish house overlooking a canal. The rooms are comfortable, and breakfast is served in a lovely room with a fireplace. Guests can expect friendly service.
➕ c2 ✉ St.-Annarei 26 ☎ 050 34 13 36 🕐 Closed Jan 🚌 4, 14

ANSELMUS

anselmus.be

A pleasant family-run hotel in a 17th-century mansion centrally situated in a quiet street. A buffet breakfast is served in the conservatory.
➕ c2–3 ✉ Ridderstraat 15 ☎ 050 34 13 74 🕐 Closed Jan to mid-Feb 🚌 All buses to Markt

DE GOEZEPUT

hotelgoezeput.be

This is a delightful small hotel in an 18th-century monastery. The rooms ooze charm and comfort; the cellar-bar is popular with locals.
➕ b3 ✉ Goezeputstraat 29 ☎ 050 34 26 94 🚌 All buses to t'Zand

GRAND HOTEL DU SABLON

hotelsablon.be

A traditional hotel with a calm ambience. The rooms offer modern facilities and guests can enjoy a buffet breakfast. The rear of the hotel was an inn 400 years ago.
➕ b3 ✉ Kopstraat 10 ☎ 050 96 02 46 🚌 All buses to Markt

HOTEL MONTANUS

denheerd.be

A romantic family-run boutique hotel in a 17th-century mansion with an interior garden. The chic rooms feel luxurious and many of them have a shared front terrace overlooking the garden.
➕ c3 ✉ Nieuwe Gentweg 78 ☎ 050 33 11 76 🚌 1, 11

HUYZE DIE MAENE

huyzediemaene.be

This very popular bed-and-breakfast has just two luxurious rooms and a sumptuous suite. The location is very central.
➕ b3 ✉ Markt 17 ☎ 050 33 39 59 🚌 All buses to Markt

MARTIN'S RELAIS

martinshotels.com

Attractive renovation of five 17th-century houses, furnished with antiques and overlooking a canal. The rooms are individually decorated with a perfect blend of the modern and old-world charm.
➕ c2 ✉ Genthof 4a ☎ 050 34 18 10 🚌 4, 14

PRINSENHOF

prinsenhof.be

This small and quiet hotel, decorated in Burgundian style, offers a free guided tour of Bruges in English.
➕ b3 ✉ Ontvangersstraat 9 ☎ 050 34 26 90 🚌 All buses to Markt

Luxury Hotels

BRUSSELS

AMIGO

roccofortehotels.com

One of Brussels' finest hotels, the Amigo is in the style of an 18th-century mansion. The staff are friendly and the rooms are elegantly furnished. It is popular with politicians and celebrities.

🔢 E5 ✉ Rue de l'Amigo 1–3 ☎ 02 547 4747 🚇 Bourse/Beurs, Gare Centrale/Centraal Station

LE DIXSEPTIÈME

ledixseptieme.be

A stylish hotel in the 17th-century former residence of the Spanish ambassador, located between the Grand Place and Central Station. The elegant rooms and suites are arranged around a tranquil courtyard and there's a fitness area.

🔢 E5 ✉ Rue de la Madeleine 25 ☎ 02 517 1717 🚇 Gare Centrale/Centraal Station

HOTEL GRAND PLACE

marriott.com

This comfortable four-star hotel with spacious rooms is right in the heart of the city, near the shopping and nightlife areas of St.-Géry and Ste.-Catherine and a short walk from the Grand Place.

🔢 D5 ✉ Rue Auguste Orts 3–7 ☎ 02 516 9090 🚇 Bourse/Beurs

STEIGENBERGER WILTCHER'S

steigenberger.com

One of the city's grandest hotels, with stylish and sumptuous rooms and suites, all the five-star amenities you'd expect, some great restaurants and perfect service. Ideal for shopaholics, it is located at the heart of Brussels' upscale shopping district.

🔢 E7–8 ✉ Avenue Louise 71 ☎ 02 542 4242 🚇 Louise/Louiza

WARWICK BARSEY HOTEL BRUSSELS

warwickhotels.com/barsey

This ultrachic hotel's rooms and suites are decorated in rich colors, with textiles and objets d'art that give a homey feeling. The restaurant, The Avenue, has a garden terrace for sunny days.

🔢 G10 ✉ Avenue Louise 381–383 ☎ 02 649 9800 🚋 Tram 93, 94

BRUGES

DE ORANGERIE

hotelorangerie.be

This small hotel has tasteful rooms in a renovated 15th-century convent covered in ivy and filled with antiques and objets d'art. This romantic boutique hotel overlooks one of Bruges' prettiest corners and in summer breakfast is served by the canal.

🔢 C3 ✉ Karhtuizerinnen-straat 10 ☎ 050 34 16 49 🚋 1, 6, 11, 16

ROMANTIK PANDHOTEL

pandhotel.com

An 18th-century carriage house hidden in a leafy square has been converted into a small and stylish hotel decorated with antiques and objets d'art.

🔢 C3 ✉ Pandreitje 16 ☎ 050 34 06 66 🚋 All buses

DE TUILERIEEN

hoteltuilerieen.com

A 16th-century mansion with cozy rooms, an indoor swimming pool and views of Bruges' beautiful Dijver canal.

🔢 C3 ✉ Dijver 7 ☎ 050 34 36 91 🚋 1, 6, 11, 16

Need to Know

Use this section to familiarize yourself with travel to and within Brussels and Bruges. The Essential Facts will give you some insider knowledge of the cities and you'll also find some language tips.

Planning Ahead

When to Go

Belgium has warm summers and mild winters. The country's northern location gives it gloriously long summer nights, perfect for enjoying outdoor cafés. The peak tourist season is July and August, when the crowds add to the buzz in Brussels but can overwhelm Bruges.

TIME

Belgium is one hour ahead of GMT, 6 hours ahead of New York and 9 hours ahead of Los Angeles.

AVERAGE DAILY MAXIMUM TEMPERATURES

JAN	FEB	MAR	APR	MAY	JUN	JUL	AUG	SEP	OCT	NOV	DEC
5°C	6°C	9°C	11°C	15°C	18°C	20°C	20°C	19°C	15°C	10°C	6°C
41°F	43°F	48°F	52°F	59°F	64°F	68°F	68°F	66°F	59°F	50°F	43°F

Spring (April to May) may take a while to arrive, but by May the weather is warmer and sunnier.

Summer (June to August) can be glorious—or cloudy and rainy.

Fall (September to November) sees mild temperatures, and there can be good, clear days, especially in September and October.

Winter (December to March) has little snow and the temperatures rarely get below freezing, but it rains frequently, sometimes accompanied by strong winds and hail.

WHAT'S ON

January *Bach Academie Brugge* music festival.

February *Bruges Beer Festival* (1st weekend).

March *Affordable Art Fair* Brussels.

April–May Brussels' Royal Greenhouses (Serres Royales) open to the public (▷ 102).

May *Procession of the Holy Blood* in Bruges (▷ 83). *Brussels Jazz Weekend.* 20km of Brussels race.

June *Brussels International Fantastic Film Festival.* Re-enactment of the Battle of Waterloo at Waterloo (▷ 106).

Brussels Ommegang historic pageant.

July *Cactus Festival* in Bruges open-air concerts. *National Day* (21 Jul) festivities in Brussels.

Mid-Jul to mid-Aug *Foire du Midi*, largest fair in Europe, in Brussels and summer fun at Brussels Beach (bruxelles-les-bains).

August *Flower carpet* (mid-Aug even numbered years) on Brussels' Grand Place. *Planting of the meyboom tree* festival in Brussels. *Brussels Summer Festival* 5-day multi-cultural music event on Place de Palais.

September *Heritage Days* Hundreds of houses and monuments open to the public free of charge in Belgium.

October *Brussels marathon.* *Nuit Blanche* art in Brussels until 3am.

Oct-Jan *Europalia*: Arts and cultural events in Brussels.

November *Ars Musica* contemporary music festival in Brussels. *Jazz Brugge* festival in Bruges

December *Christmas/Winter markets* in Brussels and Bruges. *December Dance Festival* in Bruges.

Brussels and Bruges Online

agenda.brussels
Covering concerts, shows, events, exhibitions, theatre, festivals, cinema and nightlife, this is a comprehensive and very useful guide to what's on in Belgium's capital city.

belgium.beertourism.com
Dedicated to Belgian beer and food culture, this site describes the different varieties of beer, introduces the Belgian breweries and explores the country's food.

brussels.info
Good advice on all aspects of the city, from accommodations and transportation to things to do, local customs, tips and interesting facts.

stib-mivb.be
Brussels' public transport site, covering the metro, trams and buses, has a journey planner, maps, routes and timetables.

tintinologist.org
Everything you ever wanted to know about Tintin, Belgium's comic-strip hero.

visitbruges.be
A site run by the tourist office in Bruges that has practical information, virtual walks through the city, history and recommendations for hotels, restaurants and excursions.

visit.brussels
The website of the Brussels tourist office has plenty of suggestions on how to discover the city over a weekend. Lots of practical information, a few quirky ideas, inexpensive hotel deals and a virtual comic-strip walk.

visitflanders.com
This excellent website, run by the Tourism Flanders office in Brussels, offers information on Bruges, Brussels and the rest of Flanders and also gives a bird's-eye view of the region.

TRAVEL SITES

fodors.com
A complete travel-planning site. You can research prices and weather; book air tickets, cars and rooms; ask questions (and get answers) from fellow visitors; and find links to other sites.

belgium.be
All about the country of Belgium, its history, geography and main tourist attractions, this site gives a good overview of its art, food, architecture and heritage.

INTERNET ACCESS

Hotels without WiFi are now rare in modern Brussels and Bruges. Many public spaces have Internet access and the main metro stations in Brussels, such as De Brouckère and Rogier, have Internet points or cafés. There is public Internet access throughout Bruges city center.

Getting There

INSURANCE

EU nationals receive emergency medical treatment with the European Health Insurance Card. Obtain one before visiting. Full health and travel insurance is still advised. US visitors should check their health coverage before departure. Full insurance is advised for all other visitors.

MAPS

In Brussels, street names and metro stations are marked in French and Flemish. In Bruges, street names are in Flemish only. Pick up free bus maps (and metro maps in Brussels) and timetables from tourist offices, the metro, the STIB/MIVB office in Brussels' Gare du Midi station and the bus office at Bruges rail station.

AIRPORTS AND PORTS

Belgium's principal international airport is Zaventem, 14km (9 miles) northeast of Brussels. Eurostar trains from London arrive at Brussels' Gare du Midi station. Car ferries arrive at the ports of Zeebrugge and Oostende.

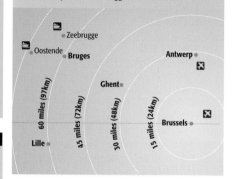

ARRIVING BY AIR

The train station is situated beneath the arrivals and departures halls of Brussels-Zaventem airport (tel 0900 70000; brusselsairport.be). Trains (tel 02 528 2828; belgiantrain.be) take passengers into Brussels Central station and to cities across Belgium and into adjacent countries. There are up to six trains an hour to and from Brussels Central (running 5.15am to 11.50pm, journey time 17 minutes, cost €9, more at weekends).

The Airport Line (tel 070 23 20 00; stib-mivb.be) bus No. 12 is an express service to the European Quarter (journey time 30 minutes, fare €5, runs until 8pm). De Lijn (tel 070 22 02 00; delijn.be) bus lines 272 and 471 run to Brussels North (Gare du Nord) station, journey time around 50 minutes, fare €3.

Metered taxis are available outside the airport but they are expensive, about €50 into the city.

Most budget airlines fly into Brussels-Charleroi airport (tel: 090 20 24 90; brussels-charleroi-airport.com), which is 36 miles (55km) to the south of the city. The Brussels City Shuttle (tel 070 21 12 10; brussels-city-shuttle.com) departs from exit 4 and buses run every 20–30

minutes to Brussels South station (Gare du
Midi) from 4.30am to 11.59pm (journey time
55 minutes, fare €17). There is also a shuttle
bus from Charleroi airport to Bruges train station between 6.25am and 11.50pm (tel: 070
21 12 10; fibco.com; journey time 2 hours 10
minutes, fare €18.20).

ARRIVING BY BUS
Eurolines buses connect major European cities
with Brussels (eurolines.eu). The international
bus station is CCN Gare du Nord/Noordstation
(Rue du Progrès 80, tel 02 669 2007). There
are direct buses from London St. Pancras
International station to Bruges, as well as frequent trains from the three main Brussels'
stations to Bruges (journey around one hour).

ARRIVING BY TRAIN
High-speed Eurostar trains from London St.
Pancras International arrive at Brussels' Gare du
Midi (journey time two hours; eurostar.com).
Trains to Bruges leave from the same station.
Thalys trains from Paris and TGV trains from
around France and ICE trains from Germany
also arrive at Gare du Midi. Trains connect many
major European cities to Brussels, and there are
trains from Germany and Holland to Bruges.

ARRIVING BY SEA
P&O Ferries operates overnight car ferry sailings
from Hull in the UK to Zeebrugge (pofer-ries.
com; journey time 14 hours). To drive from
Zeebrugge to Bruges take the N31 and N9
(25 minutes), and to Brussels the N31 and
E40 (1 hour 25 minutes).
  DFDS Seaways operates car ferries from
Dover to Dunkirk (dfdsseaways.co.uk; journey
time two hours). Take the E40 to drive from
Dunkirk to Bruges (one hour) and Brussels
(1 hour 45 minutes).
  Both P&O Ferries and DFDS Seaways cross
from Dover to Calais in 90 minutes. From Calais
take the A16 and E40 to Bruges (1 hour 25
minutes) and Brussels (2 hours).

PASSPORTS/VISAS
Always check the latest
entry requirements before
you travel, as regulations
can change at short notice.

VISITORS WITH DISABILITIES
● Few buildings in Brussels
and Bruges have facilities
for people with disabilities,
and the streets have
uneven cobblestones,
which are tough on
wheelchairs.
● The website wheelchair-
travel.org/brussels is a
helpful guide to facilities in
the Belgian capital, from
good places to visit and
accessible hotels to the
lowdown on public trans-
portation.
● To request a wheelchair-
accessible (PRM) taxi, call
Taxis Verts (tel 02 349
4949; taxisverts.be). The
waiting time can be quite
long so it is advisable to
call in advance of when it
is needed.
● Information on access in
Bruges can be downloaded
from visitbruges.be/bruges-
accessible-to-everyone-
brochure.

NEED TO KNOW GETTING THERE

Getting Around

BICYCLING TOURS

● In Bruges several companies offer bicycle tours with a guide, around the city or to the surrounding countryside, including Damme and Oostburg. One of the best is QuasiMundo Biketours (☎ 050 33 07 75; quasimundo.com). Others include the Pink Bear Bike Tours (☎ 050 61 66 86; pinkbear.be) and the Green Bike Tour (☎ 050 61 26 67).

● In Brussels, Pro Vélo organizes interesting bicycling tours with different themes (☎ 02 502 7355; provelo.org).

BICYCLES

● The best way to get around Brussels is by bicycle, but watch out for traffic. Villo! is Brussels' popular bike-sharing scheme that allows you to take a bike from one of the 360 stations in the Brussels-Capital Region and return it to another. The first 30 minutes of rental are free. A day ticket can be good value and costs just €1.60.

Getting around Bruges by bicycle is great and Damme is only 4 miles (6.5km) away, and Knokke or Zeebrugge less than 13 miles (21km). You can rent bicycles from:

● Station Brugge (blue-bike.be)

● 't Koffieboontje (Hallestraat 4 tel 050 33 80 27; adventure-bike-renting.be).

● Eric Popelier (Mariastraat 26, tel 050 34 32 62; fietsenpopelier.be; also has tandems and scooters).

● Bauhaus Bike Rental (Langestraat 133–137, tel 050 34 10 93; bauhaus.be).

● Your bike needs a ticket if you are taking it on the train. Folding bikes go free, others cost €8 for the day.

BUSES, TRAMS AND METRO IN BRUSSELS

Brussels has an integrated public transportation system of metro, trams and buses. Metro stations are indicated by a white letter M.

There are four metro lines, numbered 1 (purple), 2 (orange), 5 (yellow) and 6 (blue). The metro map shows interchange stations and the numbers of the connecting buses and trams that serve the station above ground. Underground premetro trams link Brussels-Nord and Brussels-Midi stations via Bourse.

Tickets can be bought at machines in every metro station and the largest bus and tram stops, also at newsagents. They are valid for one hour, can be used on all three modes of transport and must be validated before travel in the machines on metro platforms or inside buses and trams (stib-mivb.be; tel: 070 23 20 00). Fines can be issued for non validated tickets so ensure you use the machines.

BUSES IN BRUGES

● The heart of the city is small and walkable. However, the efficient bus network makes it easy to explore farther afield.
● Buy tickets on board or from newsstands (in which case you must get them stamped on the bus). A one-day pass (*dagticket*) is available.
● Up-to-date bus schedules are on display at the Bruges Tourist Office.

TAXIS

● In Brussels, use only official taxis, with a taxi light on the roof. They also have a yellow and blue triangle on the roof. Taxis are metered and can be called or flagged down, but are not allowed to stop if you are less than 100m (110 yards) from a taxi stand. The meter price is per kilometer and is doubled if you travel outside the city (tel 02 411 4142 or 02 715 4040).
● There are several taxi stands in Bruges, including at the train station and Markt (tel 050 36 36 49 or 050 70 75 10).

TRAINS

● Brussels has three main stations: Gare du Midi/Zuidstation, Gare Centrale/Centraal Station and Gare du Nord/Noordstation. Two other stations, Schuman and Quartier Léopold, serve the EU institutions and the headquarters of NATO. Bruges has only one station, and there are frequent buses into town.
● Tickets are sold in stations, not on the train. Special offers are available on weekends and for day trips.
● Frequent trains from Brussels run to the outlying areas and from Bruges to the coast.
● For train information, contact SNCB/NMBS on 02 528 2828; belgiantrain.be.

HORSE AND CARRIAGE

Calèches are a popular way to see the historical heart of Bruges. You can pick one up on the Markt, and the ride takes about a half hour, with a little stop at the Begijnhof. The price per cart is fixed at €50.

STUDENTS

Reductions are available on ticket prices for all state-run museums for holders of recognized international student cards.

METRO OFFERS

The most economical way to travel by Brussels public transport is to buy 10 tickets (*dix trajets*), 5 tickets (*cinq trajets*) or a 1- or 3-day unlimited travel pass, all valid on bus, tram or metro. You must get the ticket validated on the bus/tram or in the metro station.

PARKING IN BRUGES

The use of a parking disc is compulsory to park in central Bruges from 9am–8pm; parking is allowed for up to four hours and is very expensive. Several streets have been reserved for residents' parking. Visitors are encouraged to drop off their luggage at their hotel and then park the car in one of the large car parks in the city or the P Centrum car park near the train station, with a free bus service into town. Central Bruges is quite small and most of the sights are easily reached on foot. For a list of car parks see (visitbruges.be/parking).

Essential Facts

NEED TO KNOW · **ESSENTIAL FACTS**

BRUGES MUSEUMS

Many Bruges museums, except some privately owned ones, close on Monday.

MONEY

The euro is the official currency of Belgium. Bank notes come in denominations of 5, 10, 20, 50, 100, 200 and 500 euros and coins in denominations of 1, 2, 5, 10, 20 and 50 cents and 1 and 2 euros.

LOST/STOLEN PROPERTY

● Report stolen property to the police. For insurance purposes, ask for a certificate of loss.
● Brussels' central police station is at rue du Marché au Charbon 30 (tel 02 279 7979). Bruges' central police station is at Kartuizerinnenstraat 4 (tel 050 44 88 44).
● The Lost-and-Found office in Brussels is at rue du Frontispice 55 (tel 02 274 1690). Lost Property offices for public transport are at: Botanique/Kruidtuin metro station, Brussels (tel 070 220 200); Stationplein 5, Bruges (tel 050 30 23 28).

MAIL

● Stamps are available from post offices and vending machines.
● Brussels' most centrally located post office is at boulevard Anspach 1 (tel 02 226 9700, Mon–Fri 8–6, Sat 10.30–4.30).
● Bruges' Post Office is at Smedenstraat 57 (tel 022 01 23 45, Mon–Fri 9–6, Sat 9–3).

MEDICAL TREATMENT

● See page 116 for details of the European Health Insurance Card.
● Most doctors speak French and English and can visit if you are too sick to move. Visits must be paid for in cash or by check. The following hospitals provide 24-hour emergency assistance:

Medical treatment in Brussels

● Cliniques Universitaires St.-Luc, Avenue d'Hippocrate 10, Woluwe St.-Lambert, tel 02 764 1111
● CHU St.-Pierre, Rue Haute 290, tel 02 535 3111
● Hôpital Universitaire des Enfants Reine Fabiola (for children), Avenue Jean Crocq 15, Laeken, tel 02 477 3300

Medical treatment in Bruges

● Akademisch Ziekenhuis Sint-Jan, Ruddershove 10, tel 050 45 21 11
● Algemeen Ziekenhuis Sint-Lucas, St.-Lucaslaan 29, tel 050 36 91 11

MEDICINES

Pharmacies (*Pharmacie/Apotheek*), marked with a green cross, open Mon–Fri 9–6. Each displays a list of pharmacies that open outside these hours.

NEWSPAPERS

Newspapers include the Flemish *De Morgen* and *De Standaard* and the French-language *Le Soir*.

SENSIBLE PRECAUTIONS

● By law, visitors over 21 must carry a passport or ID card at all times.
● Watch out for pickpockets and bag-snatchers, particularly in crowded areas in Brussels and at stations.
● In Brussels, take a taxi at night, rather than the metro, bus or tram.
● Be careful in downtown Brussels, especially the red-light area at Gare du Nord, which can be dangerous at night, and the area near Comte de Flandre metro station, which is known for street crime.

SMOKING

Smoking is banned in public places and in most restaurants and bars.

TELEPHONES

● Many phone booths accept only prepaid phone cards, available from post offices, supermarkets, stations and newsstands.
● International calls are expensive. Rates are slightly lower 8pm–8am and on Sunday.
● The city codes (02 for Brussels; 050 for Bruges) must be used even when calling from within the city.
● To call the UK from Belgium dial 00 44, then drop the first 0 from the area code. To call Belgium from the UK dial 00 32, then drop the first 0 from the area code.
● To call the US from Belgium dial 001. To call Belgium from the US dial 011 32, then drop the first 0 from the area code.

TOILETS

Public restrooms are usually clean. Tip attendants in bigger restaurants and cafés; the amount is posted on the wall.

English is widely understood in Belgium, but if you'd like to try the local language, here are some phrases that may help. Be sure to choose the correct language—if you speak French to a Flemish person, they might be offended. Similarly, if you speak Flemish to a French-speaking *Bruxellois*, they may well reply in French with some disdain.

BASIC VOCABULARY (FRENCH)

Oui/Non	Yes/no
S'il vous plaît	Please
Merci	Thank you
Excusez-moi	Excuse me
Bonjour	Hello
Au revoir	Goodbye
Parlez-vous anglais?	Do you speak English?
Je ne comprends pas	I don't understand
Combien?	How much?
Où est/sont...?	Where is/are...?
Ici/là	Here/there
Tournez à gauche/ droite	Turn left/right
Tout droit	Straight on
Quand?	When?
Aujourd'hui	Today
Hier	Yesterday
Demain	Tomorrow
Combien de temps?	How long?
À quelle heure ouvrez/fermez-vous?	What time do you open/close?
Avez vous...?	Do you have...?
Une chambre simple	A single room
Une chambre double	A double room
Avec salle de bains	With bathroom
Le petit déjeuner	Breakfast
Le déjeuner	Lunch
Le dîner	Dinner
Acceptez-vous des cartes de crédit?	Do you accept credit cards?
J'ai besoin d'un médecin/dentiste	I need a doctor/ dentist
Pouvez-vous m'aider?	Can you help me?
Où est l'hôpital?	Where is the hospital?
Où est le commissariat?	Where is the police station?

NUMBERS (FRENCH)

un	1
deux	2
trois	3
quatre	4
cinq	5
six	6
sept	7
huit	8
neuf	9
dix	10
onze	11
douze	12
treize	13
quatorze	14
quinze	15
seize	16
dix-sept	17
dix-huit	18
dix-neuf	19
vingt	20

CONVERSATION (FLEMISH)

Ja/neen	Yes/no
Alstublieft	Please
Dank u	Thank you
Excuseer	Excuse me
Hallo	Hello
Goedemorgen	Good morning
Goedenavond	Good evening
Tot ziens	Goodbye
Spreekt u Engels?	Do you speak English?
Ik begrijp u niet	I don't understand

USEFUL QUESTIONS (FLEMISH)

Hoeveel?	How much?
Waar is/ zijn…?	Where is/are…?
Wanneer?	When?
Hoelang?	How long?
Wanneer is het open/ gesloten?	At what time do you open/close?
Heeft u…?	Do you have…?
Hoeveel kost dit?	How much is this?
Aanvaard u een kredietkaart?	Do you take credit cards?
Kunt u mij helpen?	Can you help me?
Waar is het ziekenhuis/politie kantoor?	Where is the hospital/police station?

WORDS AND PHRASES (FLEMISH)

Hier	Here
Daar	There
Sla rechts af	Turn right
Sla links af	Turn left
Rechtdoor	Straight
Een enkele kamer	A single room
Een dubbele kamer	A double room
Met/zonder badkamer	With/without a bathroom
Ik heb een dokter/ tandarts nodig	I need a doctor/ dentist

NUMBERS (FLEMISH)

een	1
twee	2
drie	3
vier	4
vijf	5
zes	6
zeven	7
acht	8
negen	9
tien	10
elf	11
twaalf	12
dertien	13
veertien	14
vijftien	15
zestien	16
zeventien	17
achttien	18
negentien	19
twintig	20
een en twintig	21
dertig	30
veertig	40
vijftig	50
zestig	60
zeventig	70
tachtig	80
negentig	90
honderd	100
duizend	1,000

WHEN? (FLEMISH)

Vandaag	Today
Gisteren	Yesterday
Morgen	Tomorrow
Ontbijt	Breakfast
Lunch	Lunch
Diner/ avondeten	Dinner

Timeline

EARLY DAYS

● Brocsella (Brussels) was first mentioned in AD695 on the trade route between Cologne and Flanders.
● In 979, Charles, Duke of Lorraine, moved to St.-Géry (central Brussels), founding the city.
● In 1459 Philip the Good, having inherited Flanders and Burgundy, brought Brabant and Holland under his control and settled in Brussels.

BRUSSELS

1515 Charles V, soon to be Holy Roman Emperor and King of Spain and the Netherlands, arrives in the city and rules his empire from here until he abdicates in 1555.

1568 A revolt begins leading to independence of the United Provinces of the Netherlands from Spain, but not of present-day Belgium, it's known as the Spanish Netherlands.

1695 French forces attack Brussels, destroying 4,000 buildings.

1713–94 Brussels is capital of the Austrian Netherlands, under Habsburg rule.

1795 Brussels is under French rule.

1815 Brussels reverts to the Dutch, after Napoleon Bonaparte's defeat at Waterloo.

1830 The Belgian Revolution leads to independence in January 1831.

1957 Brussels becomes the HQ of the EEC.

2002 Euro notes and coins are introduced.

2013 King Albert II abdicates in July in favor of his son Philippe.

2019 Brussels hosts the start of Le Tour de France.

From left to right: Napoleon; a map showing the positions of the British and French armies at the Battle of Waterloo; Europe Day celebrations in Brussels; Charles V; a man in medieval dress

BRUGES

AD800–900 Bryggja is established, named for the Norse for "mooring place."

1127 The first walls go up around the city of Bruges.

1302 Flemish craftsmen and peasants defeat a French army at the Battle of the Golden Spurs.

1473 On his press in Bruges, William Caxton creates the first book printed in English.

1488 An uprising against the Habsburg Archduke Maximilian leads to his kidnap and three months' detention in Bruges. The reprisals against the Bruges burghers begin the steady decline of the city when Maximilian becomes emperor in 1493.

1898 Flemish is officially recognized as the country's joint language with French.

1907 Port of Bruges-Zeebrugge inaugurated by King Leopold II.

2000 Bruges becomes a UNESCO World Heritage Site.

2018–2020 The Flemish Masters Project showcases great works of art at exhibitions across Flanders. 2019 marks the 450th anniversary of Bruegel's death.

TRADING SUCCESS

By the early 14th century Bruges had become one of the world's great trading cities. In 1384 Philip the Bold, Duke of Burgundy, inherited Flanders and ushered in a period of prosperity and great cultural and political changes. However, the city began to decline when Maximilian became emperor in 1493. In 1516 Genoese and Florentine traders, who had set up business ventures in Bruges under a treaty of 1395, moved to Antwerp. A further difficulty arose in 1550, when Bruges lost access to the sea, with the silting up of the inlet that is now known as the Zwin.

Index

Titles in the Series

- Amsterdam
- Bangkok
- Barcelona
- Berlin
- Boston
- Brussels and Bruges
- Budapest
- Chicago
- Dubai
- Dublin
- Edinburgh
- Florence
- Hong Kong
- Istanbul
- Krakow
- Las Vegas
- Lisbon
- London
- Madrid
- Melbourne
- Milan
- Montréal
- Munich
- New York City
- Orlando
- Paris
- Rome
- San Francisco
- Seattle
- Shanghai
- Singapore
- Sydney
- Tokyo
- Toronto
- Venice
- Vienna
- Washington, D.C.